MATH IN PRACTICE

A Guide for Teachers

Susan O'Connell

Heinemann • Portsmouth, NH

Heinemann
361 Hanover Street
Portsmouth, NH 03801–3912
www.heinemann.com

Offices and agents throughout the world

The author and publisher wish to thank those who have generously given permission to reprint borrowed material:

Excerpts from Common Core State Standards © Copyright 2010. National Governors Association Center for Best Practices and Council of Chief State School Officers. All rights reserved.

"Misinformed beliefs" adapted from *Now I Get It: Strategies for Building Confident and Competent Mathematicians, K–6*, by Susan O'Connell. Copyright © 2005 by Susan O'Connell. Published by Heinemann, Portsmouth, NH. All rights reserved.

Figure 3.8: Hundredths Disk from *Teaching Student-Centered Mathematics: Developmentally Appropriate Instruction for Grades PreK–2* (Volume 1), 2nd Edition, by John A. Van de Walle, Lou Ann H. Lovin, Karen S. Karp, and Jennifer M. Bay-Williams. Copyright © 2013. Published by Pearson Education, Inc., New York, New York. Printed and electronically reproduced by permission of the publisher.

Cataloging-in-Publication Data is on file at the Library of Congress.
ISBN: 978-0-325-07472-6

Editor: Katherine Bryant
Production: Victoria Merecki
Cover and interior designs: Suzanne Heiser
Typesetter: Publishers' Design and Production Services
Manufacturing: Steve Bernier

Printed in the United States of America on acid-free paper
20   19   18   17   VP   2   3   4   5

To Katie and Brendan, for your love and support.

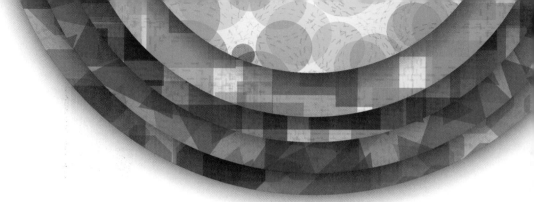

Contents

Acknowledgments

This project began with educator focus groups, and I am indebted to those educators who articulated their needs and put us on the path to developing this series. Their concerns and suggestions about how best to support elementary math teachers have guided us throughout the project.

When the scope of this project was realized, it was evident that it would take a collaborative effort to pull it off, as well as some outstanding math educators. Thank you to the very special group of authors who put their expertise onto the pages of the books in this series: Marcy Myers, Laura Hunovice, Allison Peet, Cheryl Akers, Kay Sammons, and Joan Petti Tellish. Their unique perspective about the teaching of math and their years of experience working with both students and teachers have provided countless activities, tips, and insights to guide the teaching of math K–5.

Special thanks to John SanGiovanni, who helped construct the vision of the project, worked with me to brainstorm formats, helped iron out problems, contributed lessons, and shared his vast knowledge of elementary math. As always, John's expertise is valued and I am grateful to have had another opportunity to collaborate with him.

I am so thankful to the following administrators who kindly welcomed me into their buildings to work with students, gather student work, or take photos of students exploring math ideas: Michelle Carey (Grasonville, Maryland), Louise DeJesu (Glen Burnie, Maryland), Gina Nelson (Plymouth Meeting, Pennsylvania), Donna O'Shea (Laurel, Maryland), Richelle Shelton (Cleveland, Tennessee), Debi Short (Severna Park, Maryland), Karen Soneira (Annapolis, Maryland), and Randall Stevens (Cleveland, Tennessee).

Many thanks to my colleagues who graciously contributed their ideas and expertise throughout the pages of Math in Practice: Melissa Bishop, Jeanine Brizendine,

Stacy Carson, Allison Hall, and Chris Oberdorf. Thanks, too, to the many, many K–5 teachers who supported us throughout the project. Being able to get into classrooms to try activities, capture students' thinking, and reflect on the best approaches for building students' understanding has been essential to this process. Thanks to Cheryl Wallace, Beth Doster, Alicia Kahrs, and Julie Shirer for coordinating the use of photos and student work samples from their buildings. Thanks to Stephanie Ross for the wonderful photos of students at work doing mathematics.

Thanks to Michelle Carey for welcoming us to Grasonville Elementary School for the video component of this project. It was inspiring to work with the students, seeing their excitement about math, and hearing their insights. And it was heartwarming to be welcomed so warmly into their school. Thanks to Allison Hall for the wonderful job of coordinating the logistics for the on-site videotaping. Also, thanks to the authors who facilitated lessons that day: Allison, Cheryl, Joan, John—your contribution to the videotaping made it a success.

And then there is the Heinemann team that worked tirelessly to make this project a reality. Every individual who has been a part of this project has been tremendously supportive, enthusiastic, and helpful. Special thanks to the original team, Vicki Boyd, Anita Gildea, and Katherine Bryant, who sat with me and John to craft the vision for the series. Thanks to Sue Paro, who has been a part of this project almost from the start. Her contributions in all aspects of the program's development have been indispensable. Thanks to Josh Evans, whose constant enthusiasm and insightful comments kept us moving in the right direction. Thanks to Victoria Merecki, Hilary Goff, and the production staff, who were attentive to every detail, and there have been many of them. Thanks to Suzanne Heiser for the beautiful designs. Thanks to Sherry Day, our video producer, for her vision and organization of the video of classroom lessons and to David Stirling for the incredible photos of students exploring math. Thanks to Amanda Bondi, Lauren Audet, and Sarah Fournier for their endless behind-the-scenes support. And finally, I am tremendously grateful to Katherine Bryant, our amazing editor, who has partnered with me throughout this project. She has tirelessly focused on every detail and has pushed and pulled me along through the many phases of the project.

Thanks to Brendan, Katie, Allison, and Jason for pitching in as deadlines got tight and so many tasks still needed to be done. A deep thanks to six very special math students who I know will dazzle the world with their intelligence and curiosity: Colin, Bailey, Liam, Blake, Molly, and Kellen. Their smiles and hugs remind me every day that life is about the people you love. And to Pat, who will always be in my heart.

Introduction

"What's wrong with the old way of teaching math? I learned math that way and I am just fine!" Have you ever heard that? From parents of your students? From colleagues? From family members? From friends? As we go through the growing pains of changing how we teach mathematics to elementary students, many adults think back on our own experiences as students in the math classroom and often long for the "good old days."

It is our nature to look back to the good old days with rose-colored glasses. But did everyone learn and love mathematics in those classrooms? What do you remember about math class when you were the student? What did the teacher do on a typical day in math class? What did you do? What was a typical assignment? What did your classroom look like and sound like? As I listen to teachers across the country describe their experiences in math class, I am struck by the similarity of their experiences as they recall:

- lots of memorizing
- long worksheets
- silent practice
- teacher telling how to do it
- one right answer
- one way to get the answer
- no group work
- no manipulatives.

And consider these often-heard comments about their feelings as they sat in math classrooms:

- "Math class was boring."
- "Math made no sense to me."
- "It was confusing."
- "I just didn't get it."
- "I was frustrated."
- "I felt stupid."
- "I hate math!"

The good old days? Some students got math; others didn't. Some loved math; others were frustrated and confused. And those who were good at math, who excelled in the classroom, often admit that despite being able to get the right answers they really didn't understand the math they were doing.

What does it mean to be mathematically proficient?

What did it mean to be good at math? If we memorized our math facts and could do standard algorithms and get the right answers, we felt that we were good at math, because elementary math was about memory, speed, and correct answers, right? And if we could do those things, we were rewarded with good grades. But is that true today? Are those the expectations we have for our students?

Perhaps one of the biggest changes in the teaching of mathematics in recent years is a new definition of math proficiency. We certainly agree that the computation skills we learned were important, and still are, but is that all it takes to be a mathematician, even at the elementary level? Don't we want our kindergarten students to be able to tell us why 6 is more than 3 or our third graders to compare $\frac{2}{3}$ and $\frac{2}{5}$ simply by reasoning based on their understanding of denominators? Don't we want our fifth graders to understand and be able to explain why 2.3 is more than 2.25? Although we can sometimes be heard to grumble about all that this new definition entails, when we think of it from our students' perspective, how can we deny that understanding math ideas, being able to solve math problems, and feeling confident about our math abilities are things we wish had been a part of our own experiences?

Today's math standards, including those of the National Council of Teachers of Mathematics (NCTM) and the Common Core State Standards Initiative (CCSS), assert that mathematicians need more than procedural knowledge. In *Principles and Standards for School Mathematics* (2000), NCTM expanded student expectations to include the processes of problem solving, reasoning, representation, communication, and making connections, illustrating their vision of mathematics as more than just procedures to be practiced and memorized. Mathematicians understand what they are doing and apply their knowledge and skills to solve real problems. They explain and model their thinking, reason mathematically, and connect math ideas to other math ideas and to the real world. If mathematicians solve problems, reason, communicate, model, and make connections, shouldn't those skills be developed in our math classrooms?

As the CCSS refined math expectations for students, they cited eight Standards for Mathematical Practice that also focus on the skills that allow our students to understand, use, and apply mathematics. The framers of the Common Core standards consider these practices essential to math proficiency and challenge us to integrate these eight standards into daily lessons. These practices highlight the critical connection between procedural knowledge and conceptual understanding, and, combined with the content standards, give us a balanced view of mathematics as a blend of content and practice.

The Standards for Mathematical Practice

1. **Mathematically proficient students make sense of problems and persevere in solving them.** They possess the skills and attitudes required to become effective problem solvers.

2. **Mathematically proficient students reason abstractly and quantitatively.** They see the connection between real situations and symbolic representation and can accurately represent problems with abstract, symbolic representations.

3. **Mathematically proficient students construct viable arguments and critique the reasoning of others.** They make conjectures, share insights, and justify conclusions.

4. **Mathematically proficient students model with mathematics.** They model math situations with diagrams, manipulatives, tables, graphs, and equations and use models to solve problems.

5. **Mathematically proficient students use appropriate tools strategically.** They select and use a variety of tools as they perform math tasks and solve math problems.

6. **Mathematically proficient students attend to precision.** They communicate precisely about math as well as perform accurate computations.

7. **Mathematically proficient students look for and make use of structure.** They recognize the structure of math through its patterns and properties.

8. **Mathematically proficient students look for and express regularity in repeated reasoning.** They notice repetition in mathematics and use their observations and reasoning to find shortcuts, rules, or generalizations. (National Governors Association Center for Best Practices, 2010)

Today our expectations for students go well beyond the ability to memorize math facts and perform basic computations. Although those skills are important, we recognize them as just a part of what our students need to know and be able to do. We expect our students to understand math, think mathematically, and be able to use the math they have learned.

A focus on the Standards for Mathematical Practice builds competent mathematicians who think mathematically, apply their math understandings, and develop a positive disposition toward math.

WHAT DO WE WANT OUR STUDENTS TO KNOW AND BE ABLE TO DO?

This blend of rote skills and thinking skills is not a new idea in teaching. In reading, we recognize that basic skills alone do not make you a reader. Just because a student is adept at phonics and can name sight words does not mean he can read. How many students have you seen who can call out words, but don't understand what they are reading? Without comprehension, calling out words is simply a rote process. But our challenge is to build readers, so we teach comprehension along with phonics. We explore key comprehension skills (i.e., distinguishing between main idea and detail, making inferences, identifying sequence, seeing cause-effect relationships, and so on) that allow readers to make sense of text, and we help our students develop those skills. Teaching phonics in isolation makes no sense to us as teachers; after all, reading is about meaning. We recognize the need to balance word attack and thinking skills when teaching reading, but have we found that balance in math? Have we moved beyond the basics (memorizing facts and algorithms) to help our students think like mathematicians?

Teaching facts and procedures, and hoping that understanding happens on its own, makes as much sense as teaching phonics without attention to comprehension. The result is the acquisition of rote skills on a very weak foundation of memory and with little hope for application. We want more for our students. Our students' performance on international tests shows that they are more proficient in computations than in reasoning, justifying, or problem solving (Heibert 2003) and that their performance falters when more complex situations are posed.

So, if memorizing math facts and standard algorithms does not make a mathematician, what skills are missing? Beyond procedural fluency, what do we want our students to know and be able to do?

We want our students to:

- **Understand the big ideas of math.**
  - So much of mathematics makes sense when you understand the big ideas. When students understand the counting sequence, place value, properties, and the ways in which numbers work, math makes sense to them.
- **Create models of math ideas.**
  - We want our students to act out situations, use concrete objects, draw pictures and diagrams, or use abstract symbols to express math ideas. Modeling math ideas pushes our students to think deeply about the ideas, provides a way for them to show their understandings and justify their thinking, and allows them to simplify math tasks and solve math problems.
- **Have computational fluency.**
  - We want our students to be able to use their math understandings to efficiently perform a variety of computations, including computations with whole numbers, fractions, and decimals.

- **Have a strong sense of numbers.**
  - ⊚ We want our students to develop a strong understanding of numbers that allows them to compose or decompose numbers as needed, perform computations in varied ways, make sense of various number representations, make predictions, interpret solutions, and understand when solutions make sense.
- **Understand the math procedures they do before memorizing them.**
  - ⊚ Although we still value efficient procedures, we want our students to understand what they are doing and why it works. When students explore math procedures through models and discussions, not only do the procedures make sense but students discover important ideas about how math works. Armed with understanding, students are better able to apply their knowledge to new situations or problems. By first exploring math procedures through discussions and place value models, our students develop a solid foundation that later helps them make sense of standard algorithms.
- **Understand how math ideas are connected.**
  - ⊚ Math is a series of interconnected concepts and skills, not a set of isolated skills. Seeing connections between math ideas allows students to continually build their math knowledge. As our students explore addition, they connect it to previous experiences with counting on. As they explore tools for linear measurement, they think about the fraction number lines they have created. As they explore area measurement, they reflect back on the use of arrays in multiplication. As they explore decimal subtraction, they connect the new procedure to the known procedures for whole number subtraction and decimal addition. The interconnectedness of math ideas allows our students to build on previous knowledge and discover important insights.
- **Solve a variety of math problems.**
  - ⊚ We want our students to know more than *how* to add, subtract, multiply, and divide. We want them to be able to apply math skills to real situations. We want them to know *when* to add, subtract, multiply, or divide. We want them to have a strong repertoire of skills and strategies to be able to solve complex math problems.
- **Reason mathematically.**
  - ⊚ We want our students to reason through math tasks, to analyze data, to discover insights, to test conjectures, and to draw conclusions.
- **Communicate their math ideas.**
  - ⊚ We want our students to be able to precisely explain their strategies, defend their answers, describe math concepts, summarize their findings, and explain their conclusions. We want them to communicate about math in talk and writing to process their ideas and refine their own thinking and to show us and others what they know.
- **Have a positive disposition.**
  - ⊚ We want our students to feel confident in their math abilities, to be willing to take risks, and to persevere during complex tasks. We want them to love math!

Through well-selected math tasks, we challenge students to think about math ideas, communicate their understandings, and apply math to problem situations.

How do we get there? How do we help our students meet these goals?

We recognize that the way we were taught math does not match the hopes we hold for our students or the standards that have been set for them. So, what can we do? How do we modify our teaching so our students can develop these critical skills and understandings? Many of us have begun the transition to teaching math in a new way for a new generation of students. This transition leads us through three important steps.

1. Update our beliefs about math.
2. Rediscover math content.
3. Modify our instruction to match our new beliefs and content understandings.

Considering where we are in this process allows us to figure out our next steps as we transition to become the best elementary math teachers we can be.

UPDATE OUR BELIEFS ABOUT MATH

A decade ago, I wrote about my ten misinformed beliefs about mathematics (O'Connell 2005)—those beliefs that no one actually told me, but that I believed because of the way I learned math each day in the classroom. I believed that:

1. *Practice makes perfect.* I believed that getting better was related to the amount of practice I did and that math required long sets of practice, usually in the form of worksheets.

2. *Mastering calculations is the ultimate goal of math.* I believed that memorizing procedures, algorithms, and computations, were what math was all about.

3. *Math is about getting the right answer.* I believed the important thing was getting the one right answer and doing it in the way I was told.

4. *Math is a series of isolated skills.* I learned each topic as a chapter, took a test, and then moved to the next topic.

5. *You must know basic facts before you can learn to solve problems.* I believed that because word problems were always at the bottom of the page or at the end of the lesson, they were done after computations were mastered.

6. *The first one finished wins.* Speed was valued and a part of many classroom tasks.

7. *The best mathematicians calculate in their heads.* I believed that abstract thinking was more valued than drawing models.

8. *Teachers tell us how to do math.* I saw my job as sitting, listening, and practicing what I was told to do.

9. *Math is done just in math class.* Worksheets of isolated facts filled the day rather than connections to life. Computations rarely had a context.

10. *Some people are good at math and some are not.* I believed you were either a math person or you weren't because some students just seemed to get it naturally and the ones who didn't simply got mediocre or poor grades.

Consider all of the things you thought about math. Do you still believe them? Do you see how I could have developed these beliefs about math based on how I experienced math as a student in a typical drill-and-practice classroom? Do you see the faulty thinking in my misinformed beliefs about math?

Before we begin to change our math teaching, it's helpful to reflect on our own beliefs and consider whether they should still drive our instructional decisions. If you have a positive view of math, hold on to it. If your past experiences have filled you with frustration, anxiety, or apathy about math, now is the time to get rid of those old fears and anxieties. The better you understand math and the more strategies you acquire, the quicker those old feelings will dissolve. Let's not pass along negative views of math. It's time to break that cycle. Let your students see your love of math. Let them see you take risks. Let them see you try and fail and still want to try again.

The teaching strategies we choose will form our students' beliefs about math. Will our students leave our classrooms thinking that math is all about speed and right answers, or will they have a different set of beliefs that embrace understanding, discovering, thinking, problem solving, and risk taking? Do we believe that our students can like math and succeed at math? Do we believe that math can be taught in a more effective way? Do we see the need for reflecting about the way we teach math and finding ways to make it better for our students? We recognize that modifying our teaching practices is likely to make us feel awkward and uncomfortable at times during the process, but do we believe that it is worth it to find ways to improve the elementary math experiences of our students? If so, then we are ready for the change.

REDISCOVER MATH CONTENT

It is likely that you did not learn math for understanding and yet now, here you are, expected to teach math in that way to your students. Although you were told to memorize rules, your students are asked to model and discuss the rules. That can be intimidating! You are relearning math as you teach it—this time based on understanding.

Because so many of us learned math as simply skills to be memorized, we are getting reacquainted with the skills in a new way. Why do we ask students to count by tens? What do students need to know about place value beyond naming the tens digit and the ones digit? How can an understanding of fractions help a student understand decimals? We now look at old math content in a new way. And we benefit from opportunities to think about the math ideas, discuss the meanings, and rediscover the big ideas.

MODIFY OUR INSTRUCTION TO MATCH OUR NEW BELIEFS AND CONTENT UNDERSTANDINGS

As we rethink our goals and re-explore math content to uncover fundamental understandings, we find that some of our tried-and-true lessons may not be as meaningful as we once thought. This is not about throwing out everything we have done, but about evaluating what needs to stay and what should be modified or deleted from our repertoire. This is our opportunity to identify teaching strategies that make a difference for our students and find ways to integrate them as often as possible into our classroom lessons. The following research-informed instructional strategies are highlighted throughout this book:

1. asking deep questions
2. building conceptual understanding before focusing on procedural fluency
3. making connections between math ideas
4. connecting math concepts to real situations
5. teaching problem solving and integrating problems into daily lessons
6. using multiple representations of mathematics
7. encouraging student talk and writing
8. integrating assessment into instruction
9. differentiating lessons to meet the needs of varied types and levels of students.

Each instructional strategy yields great benefits for students and can be used regardless of the grade level or math topic. Each strategy focuses on building our students' understanding of math ideas. In addition, through active learning, thoughtful discussions, and tasks that focus on critical thinking, our students gain confidence and display joy in learning math.

As worksheets and workbooks are replaced with activities in which our students explore and discuss big ideas, we witness our students loving math!

How This Book Will Help

At which step do you find yourself as you transition the way you teach math? Are you struggling with why you need to change? Are you feeling insecure about your own content understanding now that a deeper level of understanding is our goal? Are you searching for teaching strategies to match your new beliefs about math? Are you hoping to find your confidence in and a love of teaching math? Are you just trying to be the best math teacher you can be? Wherever you are in this process, this book is designed to help you become the elementary math teacher you wish you had.

This book is about teaching *students* mathematics. It is about finding ways to help our students learn and love mathematics. This book is filled with instructional strategies that enhance math learning for our students and that make our classrooms interactive, engaging, and focused on the big ideas of elementary math.

The research-informed teaching practices that are explored throughout this book have been selected to address our new definition of mathematical proficiency. You will find many references to standards, research, and the experts in the field of teaching mathematics. It is filled with teacher-tested tips and strategies to make it more useful for you.

This book is the linchpin of the Math in Practice series, focused on teaching students mathematics in grades K–5. This book contains the rationale for and explanation of a wealth of instructional strategies. It provides the foundation for the accompanying grade-level books that are filled with examples of these instructional strategies specifically related to grade-level content standards.

Each grade-level book dives into the specific math content taught at that level. These books provide you with insights about the key math ideas being taught and provide a wealth of classroom tasks that illustrate the teaching strategies highlighted in this book. You will recognize references to problem solving, math talk, differentiation, creating models, and formative assessment as you explore the grade-level tasks. You will find lesson ideas, as well as a reflective lesson in each module that includes teacher notes to give you insight about why the lesson was developed in that way or what a teacher might be thinking or doing to promote student understanding as the lesson unfolds. You will find ready-to-use activities, center ideas, assessment tools, and practice tasks. And designing your own lessons will be easier as you explore the instructional strategies and key math content discussed and illustrated throughout the books.

Math in Practice: A Guide for Administrators provides a specific view of these strategies through the eyes of a district- or school-based administrator or math coach. That book supports leaders as they work to enhance math teaching for all students within the school or district.

A wealth of online resources are included for all of the books in the series to allow you to quickly and easily access tools, templates, recording sheets, and additional resources to make your job easier. Thumbnails appear throughout the books to give you a glimpse of some of the online resources that are available. Many of these resources are in Microsoft Word to allow you to modify the template or recording sheet to meet the needs of your students, so you can easily differentiate tasks for the abilities of different learners.

Because reflection is such an important part of this process, this book includes questions for use in faculty study groups. You can use the questions to discuss these critical ideas with colleagues or simply to reflect on your own. Discussing your classroom observations, hearing the insights of colleagues, and collaboratively planning lessons help to enhance math teaching.

Another reflective tool available in the online resources is a collection of teaching videos. These short video clips of math lessons highlight the teaching strategies featured throughout the Math in Practice series. Watching the video clips, and discussing observations and insights, will help you reflect on the benefits of the strategies and gather ideas for implementing them with your students. Although you will find a wealth of lesson ideas throughout the books in this series, the hope is that through reflection and discussion, these lesson ideas become the beginnings of many more classroom activities that you develop to suit the needs of your students.

HOW THIS BOOK IS ORGANIZED

There is a great deal of overlap between the topics and strategies discussed throughout this book. As you read from chapter to chapter, you will notice key ideas resurfacing. We teach students to solve math problems by asking deep questions, encouraging them to visualize their thinking with models, and getting them talking about their methods. As they talk about their methods, we assess their understanding and make connections to other math ideas to spur insights. There is no clear point where one strategy ends and another begins. Each of the highlighted strategies is linked to the others in a variety of ways. Our goal is to integrate these strategies into our teaching in seamless ways to support our students as they explore elementary-level mathematics.

The strategies are organized under the following key ideas about teaching mathematics:

1 Step Back and Let Them Think: Letting Students Do the Thinking

This chapter focuses on the importance of getting students thinking. Sections include discussions about teaching through discovery, fine-tuning our questioning, and teaching students to think like problem solvers.

2 Build Bridges, Make Connections: Connecting Math Concepts to Each Other and to Our Students' Lives

This chapter focuses on the power of making connections to stimulate learning. Sections include discussions about connecting math concepts across the K–5 years, using problem contexts to connect equations to the real situations they represent, and connecting math to the real world through word problems and children's literature.

3 See It, Touch It, Move It: Representations in Math Class

This chapter focuses on the role of representations in our math classrooms with sections about using representations to construct meaning, using representations to solve problems, and using representations to communicate thinking.

4 Talk About It, Write It Down: Getting Students Communicating About Math

This chapter focuses on the role of talk and writing in the math classroom with sections focusing on ways to generate math talk, develop precision through the language of math, and build our students' math communication skills.

5 Watch, Listen, Adjust: Letting Students Guide Our Teaching

This chapter focuses on letting our students guide our teaching with discussions about formative assessment options and ways to adjust our instruction to meet the needs of our varied learners.

Conclusion

Most of us learned math in classrooms characterized as teaching by telling. We now realize that method sacrificed understanding for efficiency. We also recognize that our students deserve more than that. Our goal is to help our students understand the math they are doing and learn to think like mathematicians.

As the definition of math proficiency has changed, we as teachers have struggled with how to change our teaching to align with that new definition. Through the various ideas, suggestions, and tools in the Math in Practice series, we work together to rethink our beliefs about what math teaching should be, rediscover math content in a new way, and adjust our teaching to bring engagement, discovery, reasoning, and understanding into our classrooms.

 Scan this QR code or visit http://hein.pub/MathinPractice to see videos of teachers and students in action and to access additional online resources for this book. Enter your email address and password (or click "Create a New Account" to set up an account). Once you have logged in, enter keycode MIPGT and click "Register."

Study Group Questions

1. How do our past experiences as students of mathematics affect our math teaching?
2. What factors make it difficult to change math teaching?
3. In what ways have you changed your math teaching in recent years? What precipitated the changes?
4. Why might it be important to rethink or relearn some of the math content we teach?
5. How do the Standards for Mathematical Practice change the meaning of what it means to be mathematically proficient?
6. How can integrating the Standards for Mathematical Practice into daily lessons help us transform our teaching practices?

Step Back and Let Them Think

Letting Students Do the Thinking

How much thinking did you do in math class? Were you asked to think for yourself or were you asked to memorize shortcuts or find answers based on a specific procedure taught to you? For many people, math class was more about doing than thinking, yet a major focus in today's math classrooms is the development of mathematical thinkers. In this chapter, we explore ways to get our students doing the thinking, including these ideas:

- organizing classroom tasks that focus on discovery and insight rather than the teacher telling students how to do math
- using just the right questions to stimulate and stretch students' mathematical thinking
- orchestrating problem-solving experiences that develop the thinking skills and dispositions of a problem solver.

We build mathematical thinkers as we take a step back from telling how to do math and instead guide our students to think about, model, talk about, discover, and make sense of math.

What the Research, Standards, and Experts Say About Students Doing the Thinking

The National Council of Teachers of Mathematics (NCTM) (2000) emphasizes learning mathematics through problem solving, reasoning, communication, representations, and making connections. Learning math is an active process. In *Principles to Actions* (2014), NCTM recommends research-informed teaching practices that include:

• supporting productive struggle in learning mathematics
• building procedural fluency from conceptual understanding.

Through productive struggle, students are given opportunities to grapple with math ideas. They work together to observe and discuss the ideas to make sense of them. And we shift from simply having students remember the steps of a procedure to developing understanding before introducing procedures. Understanding does not develop simply by telling someone to understand. Explorations, observations, modeling, and discussions become key ways in which our students build a solid foundation of understanding, allowing them to make sense of math ideas, which has been found to be an important component of math proficiency (Bransford, Brown, and Cocking 1999). When students memorize procedures without understanding how they work, they are less likely to be able to use them flexibly and may have less retention of the procedures (Hiebert 2003).

The Common Core State Standards, through their Standards for Mathematical Practice, also emphasize the importance of developing mathematical thinkers. These standards highlight the importance of using models, discussions, and problem-based tasks to build student understanding. Standard 8 (Look for and express regularity in repeated reasoning), in particular, highlights the important role of discovery in our math classrooms. Standard 8 focuses on the importance of students seeing the repetition that occurs in mathematics, and using that repetition to make conjectures and develop rules and generalizations (Common Core State Standards 2010). We set up investigations so students can better understand math content, but in addition, our students develop the important skills of investigating, observing for repetition, making sense of their observations, hypothesizing, testing conjectures, and developing generalizations. They are learning the skills of being a mathematician.

Arousing Discovery

For many of us, classroom time was spent doing procedures. We spent little time talking about what we did and rarely dissected the steps of the procedures. Rather than making sense of them, we simply memorized rules, or shortcuts, without understanding what we were memorizing. We found correct answers, but it wasn't an understanding of math that led us to those answers. Our brains were filled with lots of rules and shortcuts that were easily misunderstood, confused, and forgotten.

There is nothing wrong with shortcuts, rules, and algorithms. Many of them can be quite helpful for getting to an answer efficiently. Mathematics values efficiency and we want our students to be able to find solutions in the most efficient ways. But we also want to be certain that our students understand these shortcuts. For that to happen:

1. We want students to be involved in *finding* the shortcuts, not just using them.
2. We want students to be able to understand, explain, and justify why they work.

When students discover rules, procedures, and concepts, they are building an understanding of how math works. Telling them how it all works robs them of the opportunity to make sense of the math they are learning. Rather than teaching lessons that focus on only the mechanics of math processes, we develop lessons that are solidly grounded in and directed toward understanding those processes. We ask students to visualize math ideas, to talk about those ideas, to put the ideas in a context, and to answer deep questions about the math. (We'll address all of these in more detail in the chapters to come.) We focus on the math in a way that allows our students to make sense of the ideas and uncover the rules for themselves. Rather than *telling* them, we help them *discover* math ideas!

DISCOVERING VERSUS BEING TOLD

In one classroom, students are told that when multiplying a number by 10, they should simply add a 0 to the number. The students practice the skill with a series of computations.

$2 \times 10 = \underline{20}$

$4 \times 10 = \underline{40}$

$5 \times 10 = \underline{50}$

$7 \times 10 = \underline{70}$

Their teacher is pleased that their computations are correct.

In another classroom, the teacher begins by posing the same computations, asking students to use base-ten blocks to find the products:

$2 \times 10 = \underline{}$

$4 \times 10 = \underline{}$

$5 \times 10 = \underline{}$

$7 \times 10 = \underline{}$

Students show 2×10 with 2 rods of 10 and see 20 as the total. They model 4×10 with 4 rods of 10 and count the rods, 10, 20, 30, 40, to find the total.

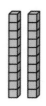 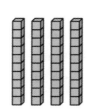

$2 \times 10 = 20 \qquad 4 \times 10 = 40$

As they record the products on the board, the teacher asks them to observe the data.

$2 \times 10 = 20$

$4 \times 10 = 40$

$$5 \times 10 = 50$$
$$7 \times 10 = 70$$

What do they notice? Why is it happening? Does it make sense? She asks them to talk with a partner about their observations and insights and then has students share their thoughts with the class.

> There is a 0 in all of the products like 20, 40, 50, 70.
>
> All of the products start with the number that is one of the factors, like 2 is in 20 and 4 is in 40.

As the teacher challenges them to explain the interesting repetition they are observing, they begin to analyze what they are seeing:

> When we did 2 × 10, we showed it with 2 rods, but that is 2 tens because each rod is 10, so that's why it's 20.
>
> When we had 4 tens, we just counted the 4 rods, 10, 20, 30 40. It's just counting by tens. 7 tens is 70, like 10, 20, 30, 40, 50, 60, 70.

The teacher asks students to predict the product of 8 × 10, and then has them check their prediction with the base-ten blocks. Were they right? How did they know what to predict? A student might say that she just knew to put a 0 behind it. The teacher probes more and asks students to explain their thinking.

> *Why would you do that? Will that always work?* (Yes, because it worked every time we did it.)
>
> *But, why?* (Because it is just 8 tens and that's 80.)
>
> *So, 8 × 10 is the same as 8 tens or 80?* (Yes, because we just moved the 8 to the tens place. It's 8 tens not 8 ones anymore, so we needed a 0 to show it was 8 tens, that's how you write 8 tens.)
>
> *Yes, the 8 is now in the tens place showing that it is 8 tens. 8 tens is 10 times more than 8 ones. That is how we record numbers using our understanding of place value. 10 times more moves the digit one place to the left!*

So which group of students gained more from the lesson? In both cases, the students were able to find the solutions. But the students who explored and conjectured throughout the task were being mathematicians. As they investigated the patterns, rather than being told a shortcut, they developed important understandings about multiplication and place value. They made connections to previous understandings (e.g., skip counting and the value of digits) and used their mathematical reasoning to make sense of their observations and develop and justify rules. And they will bring this deeper understanding to the next math task they encounter.

A FOCUS ON INVESTIGATIONS

Helping our students discover math ideas doesn't necessarily take longer than telling them how to do math, but it does take a different mindset—the mindset that students can come up with insightful observations and valid conjectures, that students can be mathematical thinkers.

Rather than *direct* teaching in which we tell our students facts and formulas and show the steps for algorithms, we focus on planning meaningful tasks, considering the classroom experiences and line of questioning that will guide our students as they explore, observe, analyze, and conjecture about the math. It is about helping them reach aha! moments during which they discover math insights and figure out how math works (see Figure 1.1). And these math insights are more easily retained, because they make sense to our students.

Consider the difference between telling students shortcuts versus helping them develop insights through investigations and discussions. You will surely recognize some of the following shortcuts and remember teachers telling you these things as their way of teaching you math. Without understanding, these rules become easily forgotten or confused. What if students explored the ideas rather than rushing to rules? Think about which approach might benefit students.

Figure 1.1 As students gather and explore data, they notice patterns in the numbers and gain insights about how math works.

Example: Adding 1

Young students often learn a shortcut for adding 1: When you add 1, it's the next number. But how might we guide students in an investigation to discover and make sense of this idea for themselves?

The teacher gives each student a ten frame and cubes or counters.

> *Show me 5 counters on your ten frame.*
> *Add 1 more. How many do you have now?*

Students count all of the counters to find the total. The teacher records *5 + 1 = 6* on the board.

> *Show me 7 counters.*
>
> *Add 1 more. How many do you have now?*

Students count all of the counters to find the total (see Figure 1.2). The teacher records *7 + 1 = 8* on the board.

The teacher continues with a few more examples. Students are then asked to talk with partners about what they notice about the equations they see recorded on the board.

> 5 + 1 = 6
>
> 7 + 1 = 8
>
> 3 + 1 = 4
>
> 6 + 1 = 7

> *What do you notice?*
>
> *What is happening when we add 1?*

Students observe the equations and look for patterns. As students share that 5 and 6 or 7 and 8 are just one number after the other when they count, the teacher might ask them to clarify what they are thinking.

> *When you add 1 it's just the next number? Why?*
>
> *Can you predict the sum of 9+1? Explain.*

Figure 1.2 Students gather data as they show 7 + 1 with counters on the ten frame and find the sum. Once data are gathered, students observe to figure out what is happening when they add 1.

Try it and see if you are right.

What would you tell someone who can't remember how to find the sum of 6 + 1?

The understanding that has been built during these discussions has eliminated the need for students to memorize +1 facts. With these insights, students can tell you 14 + 1 or 24 + 1 or 36 + 1 without any memorization (see Figure 1.3). They have discovered what +1 means.

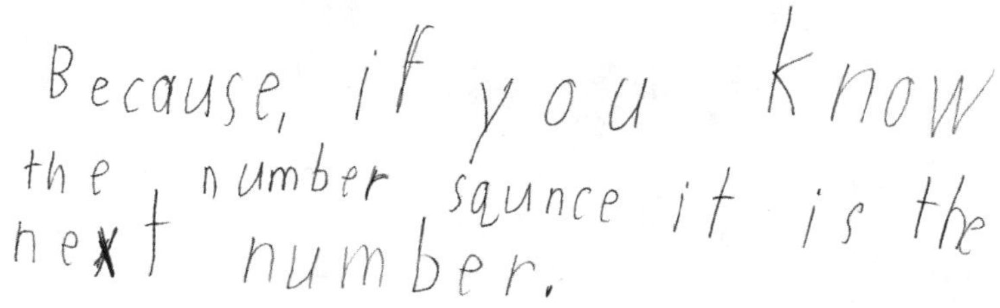

Because, if you know the number saunce it is the next number,

Figure 1.3 This student explains that "if you know the number sequence it is the next number," showing his understanding of what happens when you add 1 to a number.

Example: The Distributive Property

When introducing the distributive property, a teacher might simply ask students to remember the shortcut; that the distributive property says that $8 \times 7 = (5 \times 7) + (3 \times 7)$. One way to investigate it instead:

The teacher gives each pair of students a set of square tiles and asks them to create an area model to show 8×7, using their experience modeling multiplication in this way.

How many tiles did you use to show 8 × 7? (56.)

How do you know? Did you have to count them? (No, we could multiply 8 × 7 because it is made with 8 rows and there are 7 tiles in each row so it is like 8 groups of 7.)

The teacher records *8 × 7 = 56* on the board, then asks students to split their 8 × 7 rectangle into two rectangles (see Figure 1.4).

How many square tiles are in each?

Talk with your partner about how you can use multiplication to tell how many squares are in your rectangles. (Multiply the number of rows by the number of columns.)

The teacher records some of students' data on the board.

$8 \times 7 = 56$

$2 \times 7 = 14$ and $6 \times 7 = 42$

$3 \times 7 = 21$ and $5 \times 7 = 35$

$8 \times 4 = 32$ and $8 \times 3 = 24$

The teacher then asks students to put their two rectangles back together to form the original rectangle.

Figure 1.4 Students break apart their area model of 8 × 7 to explore the area of the two rectangles they create, discovering that 8 × 7 = (5 × 7) + (3 × 7).

Partners are asked to split the rectangle into two rectangles in a different way and record the equation for the original rectangle and the two equations to show the number of squares in the two new rectangles. Partners then observe the data on the board and their own data to discuss:

> *What do you notice? Is there a connection between the original rectangle and the two split rectangles?* (They are just parts of the big rectangle.)
>
> *Is there a connection between the original equation and the two new equations?* (One of the factors is the same in all three equations, but the other factor is split in the two new equations—like 8 becomes 2 and 6, but together 2 and 6 make 8.)
>
> *What do you notice about the products of the rectangles?* (The products of the two new rectangles are the same as the product of the big rectangle.)
>
> *Why is that?* (It's the same number of square tiles, we just moved them apart to create the two new rectangles.)
>
> *How could we use math notation to show someone that 8 × 7 is the same as 2 × 7 and 6 × 7? Talk to your partner to find a way to say this using numbers and math symbols.* (8 × 7 = 2 × 7 + 6 × 7.)

Although students may not have seen the use of parentheses before this, the teacher records the following and asks them why she may have written it in this way:

$$8 \times 7 = (2 \times 7) + (6 \times 7)$$

> *Why do you think I used parentheses?* (To show the two different rectangles we made.)

Students are challenged to gather more data to test their conjectures.

> *Do you think this will always be true? Will the product always be the same when we split one of the factors, when we split the rectangle?* (Yes, because you don't take any away or add any to it.)

Students work with partners to build a rectangle with different dimensions and then split it into two new rectangles in several ways. They are challenged to try splitting it vertically and horizontally and to write the equations to show what they found. They discuss their findings so they are ready to present them to the class.

> *How could you use this idea to find the product of 9 × 8 if you forgot it?* (You could break it apart like do 5 × 8 and 4 × 8.)
>
> *Does it matter which factor you break apart?* (No, you just have to remember to add them back together.)

The Benefits of Discovery

In both examples above, the students end up knowing the shortcut, but in the second approach, rather than being told it, they discover it. This approach has a number of benefits.

- Students are engaged in the lesson as they gather and observe data. They are doing math.
- Students use what they know about math to build new understandings.
- Students are learning the importance of observing data. They observe patterns and notice regularity, which leads them to insights.
- Students see how and when models can help them visualize math concepts and simplify math problems.
- Students develop their reasoning skills as they explore, look at evidence, make connections between math ideas, and struggle to figure out what is happening in each situation.
- Students develop communication skills as they attempt to explain what they see in the data, articulate generalizations, and justify their conjectures. They learn to listen to each other's ideas and evaluate whether the reasoning makes sense.
- Students gain confidence in their math abilities.
- Students view mathematics as an active endeavor as they solve problems and explore math ideas.

A key to helping our students arrive at the kinds of meaningful insights discovery can provide is the kind of questions we ask. Through deep questioning, we cultivate our students' reasoning skills. Let's now take a look at how our questions shape our students' learning.

Shift Away From:
Directions
Procedures
Answers

To:
• Ask Why
Ask How
Ask What
Ask for Insights

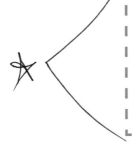

Tips for Teaching Through Discovery

Setting Up Investigations

When setting up investigations to promote discovery, consider the following steps:

1. Have students gather data through models or computations.
2. Record the data and have students observe and discuss the data with others.
3. Have students share their insights and predict based on their insights.
4. Have them test their conjecture with additional examples.
5. Have them summarize what they learned and verbalize any rules or generalizations they have uncovered.

Focus on Understanding

Initial experiences with computational procedures should not begin with standard algorithms, but with explorations, models, and discussions related to place value, properties, and an understanding of the operations. Standard algorithms are introduced after students understand the procedures.

Record Observations

Record students' observations as you explore math ideas. Use words, pictures, and numbers to show their thinking. Refer back to the ideas frequently as students build their understanding.

What's the Rule?

Encourage students to hypothesize and test rules or generalizations. Have them predict based on their rule. Was their prediction correct?

Prove It

Encourage students to justify their rules or generalizations, explaining how and why the rule works.

Discovery Journal

Following classroom investigations, have students record their insights in a discovery journal. What did they notice? Why did this happen? Encourage them to use words, pictures, numbers, and/or examples to explain what they learned.

Essential Questions to Spur Insights

1. What do you notice?
2. Why is that happening?
3. Does it make sense? Why or why not?
4. Predict (for another similar example) based on your observations.
5. Will it always work? Explain.
6. What is the rule?

Asking Questions to Stimulate Thinking

In the past, teacher talk in the elementary math classroom consisted primarily of three things:

1. directions for an assignment
2. descriptions of procedures (e.g., explaining the procedure for adding multidigit numbers)
3. asking for an answer.

Today, teacher talk sounds quite different. It has expanded dramatically as we recognize the role of what we say in guiding our students' math learning and developing their mathematical thinking. We have begun to focus intensely on the questions we ask, posing intentional and thoughtful questions that provide our students with experience contemplating, analyzing, and articulating their mathematical thinking. Our questions are carefully designed to move students who may be struggling with a concept toward understanding or to push an advanced student to delve more deeply into a concept. They are intended to challenge students' thinking and help them make connections between important math ideas. Rather than simply explaining procedures and asking for answers, we have recognized the power of refining the types of questions we ask.

What types of questions should we be asking?

- We ask *why*. We expect students to justify their answers, defend their choices, and construct arguments to prove their thinking.
- We ask *how*. We expect students to explain how they solve problems or arrive at answers, knowing not just what steps they took, but why each one made sense.
- We ask *what*. Rather than having students copy definitions of math concepts, we expect them to define and describe key math concepts in their own words.
- We ask for *insights*. We expect students to be able to observe data, notice patterns or repetition, make conjectures, and explain their insights.

By expanding the types of questions we ask, and expecting precision and thoughtfulness in students' responses, we continue to shift our focus from doing to thinking.

What the Research, Standards, and Experts Say About Asking Questions

Questions that go beyond factual recall and require our students to think more deeply about a math skill or concept engage them in the process of learning. Research shows that higher-order questions (e.g., those that ask students to apply, analyze, and reason) produce more learning than questions that focus simply on recall of information (Marzano, Pickering, and Pollock 2001). As students struggle with explaining the how and why of mathematics, they delve deeper into the skills and concepts. Leinwand (2012) contends that the best way to implement a thinking curriculum, to focus students on alternate approaches, and to create a language-rich classroom is by regularly asking questions like "Why?," "How do you know?," or "Can you explain what you did and why you did it?" And through posing questions that connect what students are learning to what they already know (e.g., "What does this remind you of?" or "What do we know about . . . ?"), we are routinely asking them to reflect on their learning, which helps them acquire new knowledge (Fennema and Romberg 1999). Questions are not just something that occur at the end of lessons, but should be a part of math lessons from start to finish to engage students, focus thinking, and promote understanding.

QUESTIONS AS AN INSTRUCTIONAL TOOL

As an instructional tool, our questions impact both the understanding of content and the development of mathematical practice. Our questions can

- guide the development of thinking ("So what might that tell you about . . . ?")
- clarify ideas ("Who can explain what parallel means?")
- challenge students' thinking ("But what if . . . ?")
- focus attention on connections ("What does this remind you of?")
- probe for insights, predictions, and solutions ("What do you notice?")
- spark student-to-student discussions ("What do you think about what Colleen said?").

We select questions to get our students thinking in varied ways about the math they are doing. The thinking necessary to answer the question "What is the value of 3 in 4,365?" is quite different than the thinking required to "explain the relationship between the values of the threes in 34,367," with the latter one pushing students to think and communicate at a higher level. Do you ask questions like those on page 22? In what ways might these questions stimulate math thinking, clarify math ideas, and accelerate your students' learning?

MAKING YOUR QUESTIONS COUNT

Talking about math with partners and teams helps deepen our students' understanding as we'll discuss in more detail in Chapter 4, but this ability to share their mathematical thinking, critique each other's ideas, work together to solve problems, and collaborate to make sense of math ideas begins with us. Ultimately, we want to hear our students making comments like:

- "I noticed . . ."
- "I think . . ."
- "I wonder why . . ."
- "I don't think that will work because . . ."
- "I changed my mind about . . ."

How do we create an environment in which students learn this language and feel safe expressing their thinking? Does it happen when students are asked to raise their hands and answer questions that are then deemed right or wrong? Does it happen when only one student is asked to answer a question and there are few opportunities for students to listen to each other or critique each other's thinking? Does it happen when expectations for precise language are lax? To pave the way for productive student-to-student discussions, consider:

- your question selection and phrasing
- who is asked to answer the questions you pose
- how you respond to students' answers
- your expectations for those answers.

Fine-tuning these areas helps us make the most of the questions we ask and stimulate productive math talk within our classrooms.

Question Selection and Phrasing

- Selecting thoughtful questions is the starting point. Avoid concentrating on questions that ask for answers only. Get students used to explaining how they came up with their answers and justifying why their answers make sense.
- Pose questions that may have more than one right answer and that require students to think and verbalize that thinking. Rather than "What is a rhombus?," consider asking, "How is a rhombus like or different from other quadrilaterals? Explain your thinking with specific examples."
- Be specific in what you'd like students to talk about. Rather than asking students to tell you about a prime number, you might get more precise responses if you asked them to tell you about how a prime number is different from a composite number, or to use a model to help them explain the difference between prime and composite numbers, or possibly to use specific words like *factors* and *product* in their explanations.

Questions can ask students to . . .

CLARIFY IDEAS
Can you restate that in your own words?

Are you saying . . . ?

What specific words might make your explanation more precise?

How could you model this problem or concept?

RECALL IDEAS
What is a ____?

What does ____ mean?

What are the characteristics of ____?

Describe a ____.

continues

COMPARE AND/OR CONTRAST IDEAS OR CONCEPTS

How is _____ like _____? How is it different?

What are the similarities between _____ and _____?

What are the differences between _____ and _____?

CONNECT IDEAS TO OTHER IDEAS

What does this remind you of?

When have we seen something like this before? How is it like what we are doing now?

What do those numbers represent? How are they connected to the problem?

What are some real-world examples of _____?

How could you use this math idea in your life?

How is this related to what we did last week?

EXPLAIN A PROCESS

What steps did you use to _____?

How do you . . . ?

How will you solve this problem?

JUSTIFY A DECISION, SOLUTION, OR PROCESS

How might you prove that your answer is correct?

Why did you do it that way?

Why is that an appropriate strategy to solve the problem?

Why did you choose that tool?

Do you agree or disagree? Why?

Which way is more efficient? Why?

Why do you believe . . . ?

Is that always true? Explain. (Can you use representations to prove it?)

OBSERVE AND DRAW CONCLUSIONS

What did you notice about _____?

What observations did you make?

What repetition do you see? Can you explain it?

What do you still wonder about?

What conclusions can you draw?

Is there a rule or generalization here? Explain.

Will it always work? Why or why not?

PROBE FOR FURTHER IDEAS

How could we build on that idea?

What is your plan for using that to solve this problem?

Who can answer Brendan's question?

REFLECT ON THINKING (METACOGNITION)

How did you figure that out?

Did you get stuck at any point? If so, how did you get unstuck?

What were you thinking?

What was difficult about that concept?

ENCOURAGE STUDENT-TO-STUDENT TALK
AND RESPONSE TO OTHERS' IDEAS

Will Allison's plan work?

Do you agree with Jason?

Whose partner said something interesting? Share it with us.

Can someone restate what Bailey said?

SUMMARIZE IDEAS

Can you summarize what you learned?

What are the key ideas?

What did you discover?

Who Is Answering Our Questions?

- Avoid the traditional approach in which students raise their hands and only one student is called on to answer the question. Instead, use turn-and-talk strategies to get all students answering questions and sharing ideas (see Figures 1.5 and 1.6). When one student answers a question out loud, it stifles others who may have a similar answer or relieves those who did not have an answer or even think about the question being asked. Turn-and-talk strategies, on the other hand, engage all students in the discussions and provide all students with opportunities to practice putting their ideas into words before sharing them with the whole class.

For more on the value of partner talk, see Chapter 4.

- Avoid calling on students randomly and asking them to immediately share their ideas with the class without giving plenty of thinking time first. Anxiety increases rapidly when students know they can be called on at any minute without an opportunity to process their ideas. Wait time and opportunities to share with a partner before sharing their ideas with the class allow students to process their ideas, try out their thinking, and, ultimately, make more meaningful contributions to class discussions.
- Listen as students share ideas with partners and have a plan for the order in which you will ask students to share their ideas in the class discussion. Allow students who may struggle with concepts to share their ideas early in the discussion so they feel a part of the discussion and can contribute relevant ideas. Scaffold ideas so you are able to make connections from one to the other.
- Encourage student-to-student discussions by asking students to respond to each other's questions or to comment on each other's thoughts, rather than the teacher being the sole provider of questions and judge of responses.

Raise Your Hand	Turn and Talk
One person answers.	Everyone answers.
Students can be daydreaming or completely unfocused on the topic.	Everyone is refocused on the topic as they are asked to talk to partners about it.
Students who do not know the answer are embarrassed.	Students at all levels can share ideas and get ideas from a partner.
Students share their initial thoughts.	Students have time to process ideas as they talk with partners, allowing more developed ideas to be shared.
When one person shares an idea, others' answers (if similar) become irrelevant because they weren't called on first.	All students share their ideas simultaneously.
Classroom discussions can be brief and weak.	Classroom discussions are deepened because all students have thought about the ideas and are better prepared to contribute to the discussions.

Figure 1.5 Comparing hand-raising and turn-and-talk approaches shows the advantages of the latter.

Figure 1.6 Rather than calling on one student to answer his question, the teacher asks students to share with partners, engaging everyone in thinking about the math idea.

How We Respond to Students

- Create an environment in which students are willing to take risks and offer comments even if they are not sure of their correctness.

- Demonstrate to students the importance of listening to each other by asking them to restate, elaborate, or agree/disagree with each other's responses. Encourage them to ask their own questions to their classmates.

- Ask students "Why?" regardless of whether their answer is right or wrong. Be willing to refrain from declaring answers right or wrong—so that students can ponder ideas and come back to them later with additional insight. Students begin to see that reasoning and justification, rather than the teacher's approval, determine whether an answer is right or wrong.

- Ask follow-up questions to clarify ("What do you mean by . . . ?"), probe ("Is that always true?"), or extend students' thinking ("What if . . . ?"). By challenging students to elaborate on their ideas, we are helping them see what we value—their thinking rather than just an answer.

- Model that even the teacher does not always have the answer and may need to observe, investigate, and amend her thinking to find the answer.

Expecting Precise Answers

- Expect precision in students' responses. If you ask them to justify answers, expect them to clearly prove their point with math data, reasoning, or models (see Chapter 4 for more detail). If you ask them to explain how they solved a problem, expect them to explain all their steps, not just give a general comment about how they did it.
- Ask for more precision as needed. Rather than accepting vague or general responses, ask students to clarify and add precision. Consider questions like "What more can you add to that?" or "Is there an example that would help us understand?"
- Ask other students to elaborate on responses. "Who can add to Megan's response?" "What more can you tell me about exponents?"
- Ask students to use precise vocabulary in their responses. "You said a rectangle has 4 sides. What math term can you use for a 4-sided figure?" Or ask students to use certain vocabulary or ideas as they explain their thinking (e.g., "Tell me about a square, being sure to mention what you know about the vertices and sides").

USING QUESTIONS TO PROBE STUDENTS' THINKING

Although at times we might ask a single question, it is more likely that our questions are woven together to become a series of prompts that probe for different perspectives or deeper understanding. As a student responds to an initial question, a follow-up question probes a bit deeper or asks for an explanation, connection, or justification.

INSIDE THE CLASSROOM

The teacher poses 16 − 9 = ___ and asks students to discuss with partners how they would find the difference. As students talk with partners, the teacher listens to their strategies and determines who she will ask to share, asking those with more basic methods to share first.

How would you and your partner solve it, Danny? (Draw 16 circles and cross out 9 of them.)

Class, do you agree or disagree? Would that show subtraction? (Yes.)

Why? (Crossing out shows taking away and that is what subtraction is.)

$$16 - 9 = 7$$

Ø Ø Ø Ø Ø Ø Ø Ø ○
○ ○ ○ ○ ○ ○

The teacher records ideas as she prompts students for explanations.

Did someone think about it in another way? (We could make a chain of 16 cubes and a chain of 9 cubes and see how much longer the 16 chain is.)

Will that work? Can you explain? (Yes, because if you line them up you can compare and see which is more and how much more. Or, Subtraction doesn't have to be taking away, it can be comparing.)

Can you give me an example of when subtraction is comparing? (If Lisa scored 16 points and Kathy scored 9 points and we want to know how many more points Lisa scored, we can do 16 − 9 to find out.)

$$16 - 9 = 7$$

Did anyone think about it another way? (We thought about addition and said 9 + __ = 16 and knew 9 + 7 = 16.)

Would it make sense to add for this problem? Why? (No, because it has a minus sign.)

What do you think about that? (We disagree, you could add because addition is the opposite of subtraction, so if you know the addition fact you can look for the part that is missing and that's the answer, so you can think 9 plus what equals 16.)

$$16 - 9 = 7$$

$$9 + \underline{7} = 16$$

Did someone think about it another way? (We could take 6 away and then take 3 more away.)

Why would we do that? (So it would be 9 altogether that we took away.)

How does it help you to take 6 first? (Because we know that would leave us with 10 and 10 − 3 is 7.)

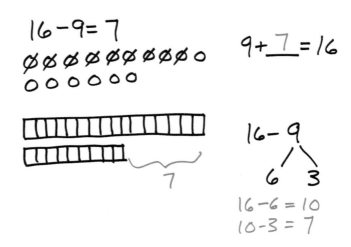

Did anyone think about it in a different way? (We took 10 away and then put 1 back.)

Does that method make sense? Turn to your partners and talk about it. Are there any other methods that were shared that remind you of that thinking? (The one with the circles when you crossed off 9.)

How is Rita's method like that one? (If you crossed off all 10 and then put 1 back, it would be like subtracting 9.)

But why would you subtract 10? (It's easier, you just know it's 6.)

But 16 − 10 = 6. Is that the answer? (No, because you have to add 1 to it because we took away 1 too many, 10 is 1 more than 9.)

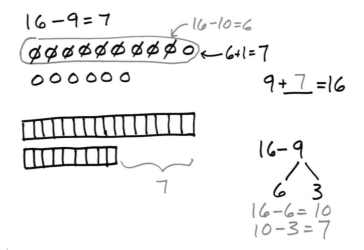

In Chapter 3, we will talk more about the value of representations to support students as they discuss and make sense of math ideas.

Look back at all of the methods and observe the sums. Tell your partner what you notice. (7 is the difference no matter how we did it.)

Is there just one way to think about 16 − 9? (No, all of these ways work because they all are subtraction.)

Even when we added and did 9 + ___ = 16? (But we looked for the part that was missing, so it is like subtraction.)

By prompting students to share their strategies and continually probing with follow-up questions, the teacher highlighted key ideas and made connections between different strategies. The teacher was able to facilitate a productive discussion about possible subtraction methods and involve all students in the discussions, either through partner sharing or sharing with the whole class.

Perhaps the most important component of planning an effective math lesson is the careful crafting of questions to guide students' thinking throughout the lesson. Jotting down these questions, and anticipating students' responses, helps us focus our planning on the learning goals of the lesson. Constructing our questions prior to the start of the lesson helps us identify a line of questioning that we believe will move students toward these learning goals. And considering how students might respond to the questions pushes us to think about how we might respond to their comments to clarify, refocus, or extend their learning. But students may not respond in the way we anticipate. The actual questioning during the lesson should be flexible to adapt to the insights or misunderstandings that occur.

As you explore the grade-level books, you will find questions throughout the lessons. The questions have been selected to guide students' thinking and involve them in productive discussions about the topic.

Through our questions, we are able to guide students' thinking by linking to previously learned ideas or making connections between related content. We are able to advance their learning as we continue to push their thinking with questions like "How?," "Why?," and "What if?" And we are able to assess the depth of their understanding. Through carefully chosen questions, we create mathematical thinkers.

For more on questioning as an assessment tool, see Chapter 5.

Focus on Thinking Like a Problem Solver

To be effective problem solvers, our students need more than computational skills. We are well aware that many students can add, subtract, multiply, or divide when given equations to solve, but those same students, when faced with problem tasks, have no idea how to solve them. Effective problem solvers are thinkers. They

- navigate their way through a multistep process from initially reading the problem to ultimately finding a solution

- choose from a broad repertoire of strategies to select ones that work for particular problems
- make a string of decisions, selecting appropriate data, choosing a reasonable operation, shifting strategies as needed, and determining the reasonableness of solutions
- possess a problem-solving disposition that allows them to take risks, collaborate, and persevere even when challenged with difficult tasks.

Along with content understanding and computational fluency, our students need these problem-solving skills and dispositions to truly use mathematics.

UNDERSTANDING THE PROCESS

Although all problem solvers follow a process of understanding the problem, identifying needed information, choosing an appropriate strategy, and then trying and checking their solutions (and maybe going back to choose a different strategy or adjusting the one they have) (Polya 2004), this does not mean that students follow the same steps or use the same strategies. Good problem solvers are aware of what they are doing. They think about their progress and adjust their strategies as they move through the process of solving problems (Bransford, Brown, and Cocking 1999).

The ability to move through this process, continually applying understanding of math concepts and expertise with math skills, allows our students to effectively solve math problems. But this process is not intuitive for many of our students. They must be taught ways to comprehend problems, identify important data, select appropriate strategies, and evaluate the reasonableness of answers. Through ongoing problem-solving experiences, rich discussions, the construction of models to make their thinking visible, and the justification of their own strategies as well as the critiquing of others' strategies, they develop into effective problem solvers. Our goal is to help each student learn to think like a problem solver, to understand and become more proficient at moving through the process of solving math problems.

Understanding the Problem

Many students jump right in to solve problems before they stop to comprehend the problem. Without an understanding of the problem itself, the entire process falls apart. Having students retell the problem in their own words, or visualize the problem with objects or diagrams, challenges them to think about the problem and make sense of what is being asked.

- What is the problem about? Can students restate it in their own words?
- What is happening in this problem? What do students know and what do they need to figure out?
- Can students visualize what is happening in the problem?

During reading lessons, when we want to check for understanding of a passage, we would not ask a student to reread the passage for us, because we know that would only tell us that they can read the words, not that they understand what they are reading. And yet, for many years in the math classroom, we have asked students to underline or read the question in a word problem, thinking that indicates understanding. Our students learn quickly how to find a question mark and underline that sentence, needing no comprehension to do this.

> There were 8 elephants.
> There were 9 eagles.
> There were 12 sparrows.
> <u>How many birds were there?</u>

> Liam had 3 liters of lemonade to sell at his lemonade stand.
> He sold $2\frac{1}{4}$ liters on Monday.
> On Tuesday, he sold $\frac{1}{2}$ of what he had left.
> <u>How much lemonade did he sell on Tuesday?</u>

Simply underlining a sentence does not mean that students comprehend what is happening in the problems.

Do you have students who would add all of the numbers in the first problem, not considering which were birds?

Would just knowing that we needed to find out how much lemonade Liam sold on Tuesday be enough to know how to solve the second problem?

Students must understand what is happening in problems to be able to solve them. <u>Understanding word problems involves reading comprehension with an overlay of math understanding.</u> Two significant comprehension strategies are <u>retelling and visualizing.</u> By restating ideas in their own words or creating pictures or diagrams of problem situations, our students work to gain a deeper understanding of math problems so they are then able to identify the information and strategies that lead to the solutions.

For Comprehension: retelling visualizing

RETELLING THE STORY/RESTATING THE PROBLEM

After reading the problem, have students turn and retell the story to a partner. Have a few students retell the story for the class.

Pose questions to delve more deeply into the story.

> *Did we miss anything important in the story?*
> *What are we trying to find out?*
> *Do we have what we need to solve it?*
> *So, what do we need to do? What is happening in this story (putting things together, comparing things, dividing a quantity into equal groups)?*

Graphic organizers, like the Beginning/Middle/End organizer used in primary classes (see Figure 1.7), help some students retell the story. Students consider what they knew at the start of the problem, what action happened during the problem, and how the problem ended. Particularly for problems in which unknowns are in different positions, this organizer helps students makes sense of story events and then transfer that understanding to a math equation for solving the problem.

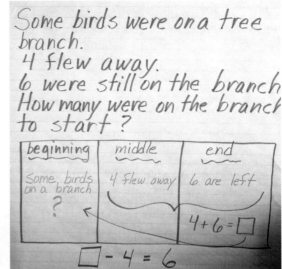

Figure 1.7 As students discuss the problem, the teacher records their ideas on the organizer as they build the equation ___ − 4 = 6, making sense of the problem even with an unknown at the start of the problem. The teacher then asks questions, as students work with counters, to make connections to addition as they discover that adding the birds that flew away and the ones still on the branch yields the birds that were on the branch to start.

Another useful strategy for retelling is to remove the data—the numbers themselves—from a problem.

At times, the data in a problem distract students from the story, particularly when the data are complex (e.g., multidigit numbers, fractions, decimals).

Consider the following problem:

> Colin and Bailey went strawberry picking. Colin picked $3\frac{1}{3}$ pounds of strawberries and Bailey picked $2\frac{3}{4}$ pounds. How many pounds of strawberries did they pick?

Have students retell the story without the data first. Colin and Bailey were picking strawberries and we want to know how many they picked together. Removing the data helps students focus on what is happening in the problem: we are combining the amount of strawberries each child picked to find the total amount they picked. Only after students recognize addition as a way to find the total do they consider the data and how they fit into the story, building their addition equation with the mixed numbers.

Visualizing Problems to Make Sense of Them

Visualizing a problem helps students make sense of what is happening in it. It helps them better understand the problem and often leads to them identifying the operation that makes sense to solve it. Visualizing problems takes on many forms, including:

- acting out the problem
- using objects to show the problem
- using math tools like part-part-whole mats or number lines

- creating pictures or diagrams to represent the problem, from circles to sticks and dots to bar models to tree diagrams
- using charts or tables to display the problem data.

Students might draw apples to find the solution to a simple addition problem (see Figure 1.8), or create an array to find out how many rows of flowers there are when there are 21 flowers and 7 in each row (see Figure 1.9). In each case, by creating a model, students are able to see the problem and gain insight into both the problem situation and a possible solution path.

How Many Apples?

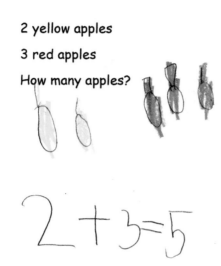

2 yellow apples

3 red apples

How many apples?

$2 + 3 = 5$

Figure 1.8 Drawing the apples allows the student to visualize and solve the problem.

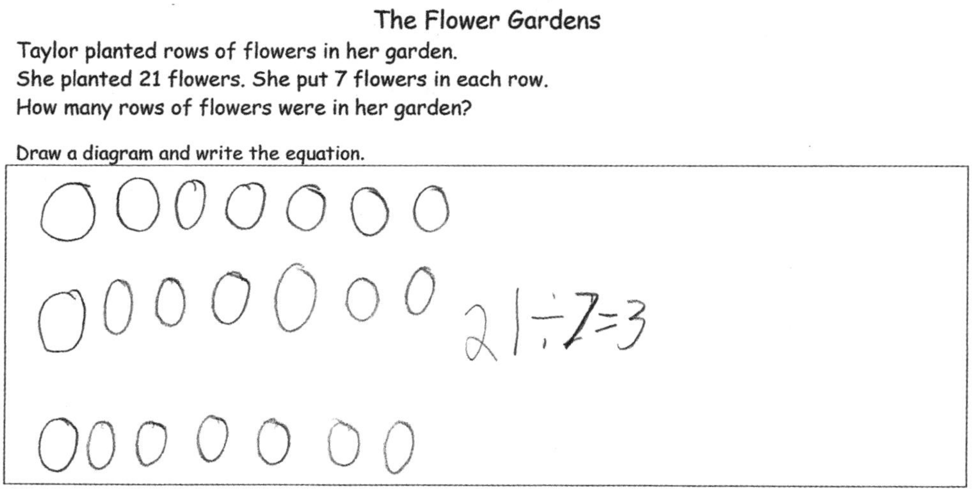

The Flower Gardens

Taylor planted rows of flowers in her garden.
She planted 21 flowers. She put 7 flowers in each row.
How many rows of flowers were in her garden?

Draw a diagram and write the equation.

$$O O O O O O O$$
$$O O O O O O O \quad 21 \div 7 = 3$$
$$O O O O O O O$$

Figure 1.9 By creating a model with 7 flowers in each row and counting to 21 total flowers, the student clearly sees there will be 3 rows of flowers.

For more on understanding the meaning of operations through problems, see Chapter 2.
For more on drawing models to solve problems, see Chapter 3.

Multiple Reads for a Variety of Purposes

Skillful problem solvers read word problems more than once. They may read the first time, ignoring the numbers, to get a general sense of what is happening in the problem, such as whether something is being added to, separated, or compared. They may read it again to see how the numbers fit in and then make a model to represent it. After solving, they go back and read it again to make sure their answer makes sense.

> First read: What is happening? Can I retell it?
> Another read: How do the numbers fit in? How can I show it?
> Read it again: Does my answer make sense?

For two-step problems, the multiple reads might be:

> First read: What is happening? Can I retell it?
> Another read: How can I get started? What should I do first?
> Read it again: What was I trying to find out? What should I do next?
> Read it again: Does my answer make sense?

Continuing to refer back to the problem, rereading it for a different purposes throughout the problem-solving process, reminds students that problem solving is all about understanding the problem situation.

Identifying Necessary Information

Once students understand what they are being asked to solve, they make decisions about what information is needed or not needed to solve the problem. In the past, students have often been asked to circle the data in the problem, resulting in students simply circling the numbers that appear among the words of the problem. Just because numbers appear in a problem does not mean they are needed to solve it (see Figure 1.10). An important extension is to have students tell what data are needed to solve the problem, including what the data represent and why they are relevant to the problem. Rather than simply circling data, we expect students to be able to justify the data that are needed and explain why.

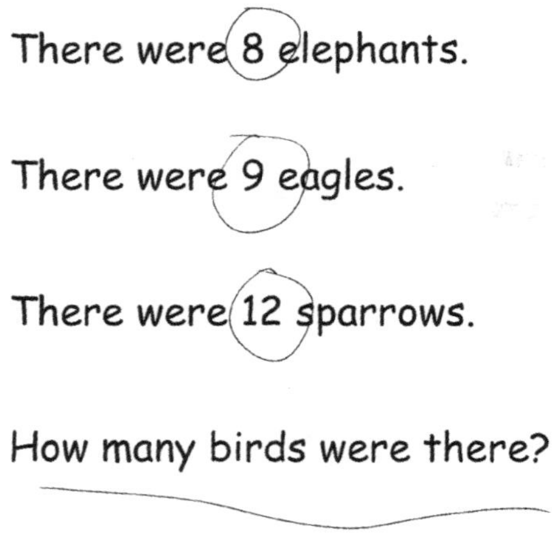

There were 8 elephants.

There were 9 eagles.

There were 12 sparrows.

How many birds were there?

Figure 1.10 This student simply circled numbers and underlined the sentence with the question mark.

For the problem in Figure 1.10, we want a student to be able to tell us something like this: "We need the 9 and 12 because there are 9 eagles and 12 sparrows and they are birds and we want to know how many birds there are. We don't need the 8 because it is 8 elephants and elephants aren't birds, so we wouldn't count them."

With an understanding of the problem, students are able to identify and justify needed data.

ARE THERE ANY CONDITIONS?

Understanding necessary information to solve a problem often involves identifying conditions in the story. Consider the following problem:

> Molly's pastry shop baked these tasty treats:
>
> 120 candy cane cookies
>
> 125 gingerbread men
>
> 55 apple pies
>
> 65 pumpkin pies
>
> Molly rolled out the crusts for the pies. The apple pies each needed 2 crusts. The pumpkin pies only needed 1 crust. How many crusts did she need to roll?

It is not enough to know the number of apple pies and pumpkin pies baked that day, but is also important to know there are 2 crusts needed for an apple pie and just 1 for a pumpkin pie. This data did not appear with the other problem data in the list of pastries, but are equally important to solving the problem.

IDENTIFYING MISSING DATA

At times, important data are not in the problem at all. In two-step or multistep problems, data may be missing and must be determined before the students can continue with the problem.

> Blake had 3 sheets of stickers with 5 stickers on each sheet and Anna had 4 sheets of stickers with 6 stickers on each sheet. How many stickers did they have together?

To solve the problem, we need to find the total number of stickers that Blake and Anna have, but we don't know how many stickers each child has. To find the total of their stickers, we must first figure out how many each child has.

When thinking about problem data and determining what is necessary to solve the problem, have students consider:

- What information will help me find the solution?
- What information should I disregard because it won't help me get to the solution?
- Are there any conditions in the problem that I need to consider to solve it?
- Is there any needed information that is not stated in the problem? How can I find it?

Students as Thinkers: Identifying Data

In the past, students have been asked to circle needed data. Taking this a step further and asking them to justify their decisions helps us check their understanding and makes their reasoning visible to others in the class.

- Ask students to turn and tell a partner what data are needed to solve the problem and to justify why those data are needed.
- Ask students to turn and tell a partner what data are not needed to solve the problem and to justify why they are not important to the problem.
- Allow students to debate their ideas.
- Consistently reinforce that needed data are connected to the question you are being asked to solve.

Developing a Plan

Armed with an understanding of the problem and the pertinent information, our students are challenged to devise a plan to solve it. This is not a rigid, memorized sequence of steps; problem solving is about decision making based on the particular problem. We want students to be asking themselves questions such as the following:

- What is a good plan for solving this problem?
- Should I add, subtract, multiply, or divide?
- Should I make a table to allow me to see patterns or other relationships between the data?
- Would a picture or diagram simplify the problem?
- Could working backward help me find the solution?
- Would organizing the data in a systematic way help?
- What other strategies might help me solve this?

For many problems, students decide which operation makes sense with the problem situation and then create an equation that represents that situation. Although this may seem like a simple skill, it is one that many students struggle with throughout the elementary years. To choose the appropriate operation, our students must fully understand the problem, know which data are appropriate, and understand the operation that makes sense to solve the problem.

We take a closer look at helping students decide which operation makes sense as we explore using problem contexts to better understand the meaning of math operations in Chapter 2.

Students may choose other strategies for finding solutions such as making tables, finding patterns, making organized lists, or working backward. These strategies give them many more options for solving the wide variety of math problems they face. We'll return to the topic of developing problem-solving strategies later in this chapter, on page 43.

Try the Plan

As students execute their plan, they are always thinking about whether it is working in the way they had hoped.

- Do I feel like I am moving closer to an answer?
- Is this making sense with the problem?

Partner talk as they implement strategies allows students to reflect on their progress together. Class time-outs, brief pauses during class problem-solving experiences, are sometimes helpful when we notice many students becoming overly frustrated or hitting a dead end. A quick time-out to engage in class sharing provides a helpful break to refocus students, discuss possible approaches, and promote perseverance. Tips or suggestions from classmates spur ways for students to get unstuck, readjust their strategies, or consider alternate paths. Solutions to the problem are not shared, and the ideas are student generated. After a brief pause, students resume their problem solving with a few new considerations and renewed energy.

Check for Reasonableness

Throughout the problem-solving process, students should be aware of whether their work is making sense. As they consider partial or final solutions, they make judgments about the reasonableness of their findings.

- What was the problem situation? What was I trying to figure out?
- Does this answer make sense with that problem?
- Does this answer make sense with the data?
- If not, what else could I try?

Some students simply do not check for reasonableness. They begin with the problem context, replace the context with an equation (decontextualize), and then solve the equation, never looking back at the context. When this happens, they often overlook unreasonable answers (see Figure 1.11). Both decontextualizing (removing the context) and recontextualizing (referring back to the context) are important aspects of the problem-solving process, and yet many students simply solve the equation and forget about the original context.

We can help students prepare to assess the reasonableness of answers at the end of problem-solving tasks by considering, at the start of the tasks, what kinds of answers would be reasonable.

- Estimating answers prior to solving the problem gives students something to compare to as they test their answers for reasonableness.
- Writing a problem statement, with the answer missing, helps students focus on the task prior to solving the problem. Once they solve the problem, they record their solution in the blank, and read the full statement to view their answer in context. For the problem:

    > There were 16 turtles sunning themselves on a log. Some of them slid off the log into the water. There were 12 turtles still on the log. How many turtles slid into the water?

    > Students begin by discussing the problem and then writing: ___ *turtles slid into the water.*

Plants in the Parks

The Parks Department bought bushes to plant in the city's parks. The table below shows the types of bushes and how many of each type were bought.

Type of Bush	Total Amount Bought
azalea	249
rose	125
holly	257
mums	285

They decided to plant the same number of holly bushes in each of the city's 3 parks. How many holly bushes were planted in each park?

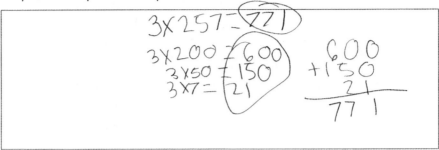

$$3 \times 257 = 771$$

$$3 \times 200 = 600$$
$$3 \times 50 = 150$$
$$3 \times 7 = 21$$

$$\begin{array}{r} 600 \\ +150 \\ 21 \\ \hline 771 \end{array}$$

Which operation did you use to solve the problem? Why?

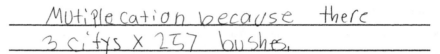

Mutiplecation because there 3 citys X 257 bushes.

Figure 1.11 Although a total of 257 holly bushes were purchased and then split among 3 parks, this student finds that 771 bushes were planted in each park. Her difficulty stems from not understanding the problem data, and she does not refer back to the problem to see if her answer makes sense.

- Labeling answers with specificity helps students test for reasonableness. Rather than labeling answers as "strawberries" when everything in the problem relates to strawberries, labeling it as "_____ pounds of strawberries picked by both children" maintains the problem context and allows students to refer to it as they consider the reasonableness of their answer.

Reflecting on the Process

Our goal is to help our students think like problem solvers. Stopping to reflect on the process after solving a problem allows them to think back on what they did and reflect on the decisions they made. By verbalizing the operation they chose and why it worked for that problem, or sharing a way they got stuck and what they did to get unstuck, they are recognizing their own thinking (metacognition) and gaining confidence in their abilities. Consider post-task reflections in which students:

- are asked to present and explain their approach and answer
- are challenged to justify their answer and method
- are asked to share where they may have gotten stuck and how they got unstuck
- are given a wrong answer/approach and asked to discuss and debate why it does not work for the problem.

DEVELOPING PROBLEM-SOLVING STRATEGIES

Strategies are ways that students get to solutions. Elementary students might add, subtract, multiply, or divide to solve problems. They might draw diagrams, make tables or organized lists, look for patterns, or reverse their thinking to work backward toward the solution. Students who understand varied ways to find solutions are able to use the strategies flexibly, as needed depending on the problem.

Understanding, Not Key Words

Problem solving is not a rote skill. To solve problems, students make a series of decisions based on their math understanding. In the past, textbooks often attempted to simplify this task by offering key words that, when memorized, would simply tell a student what operation to use or how to solve the problem. This technique has not helped our students for two major reasons.

1. Simply looking for a word leads to lots of errors and misunderstandings. Key words can appear in the problem but are not meant to indicate the operation, and key words may not appear at all.

2. It gets in the way of students really understanding how to choose appropriate operations. The decisions are based on rote memorization of a list of key words, rather than real understanding.

Consider the typical key words for addition. When a student is told that *altogether* or *in all* tells them to add, what do they do for this problem?

> There were 13 brown dogs and 14 black dogs. How many dogs were there?

Neither key word appears in the problem.

And when students spot a key word, they often disregard everything else in the problem.

> Juan and Olivia picked $2\frac{3}{4}$ cups of strawberries altogether. They ate $\frac{1}{2}$ cup on the drive home. How many cups of strawberries did they have when they got home?

Although the word *altogether* appears, it is not intended to be an indication of the operation, and yet many students quickly add the two quantities in the problem.

Or what about this problem that mentions what is left?

> Caroline made a liter of tea. She drank $\frac{1}{4}$ of it on Tuesday. On Wednesday, she drank $\frac{1}{2}$ of what was left. How much did she drink on Wednesday?

Students often mistakenly subtract to find the solution, basing their decision on the words *what was left*, and yet this is a multiplication problem ($\frac{1}{2} \times \frac{3}{4}$).

Rather than relying on key words, which can often be misleading or unhelpful, we focus on helping our students think, by exploring the situations (the actions or relationships) that indicate each operation. These situations, or problem structures, help our students identify the operation that makes sense for a given problem.

Problem 5

For more on using problem structures to identify operations, see Chapter 2.

Building a Repertoire of Strategies

Our goal is to build a wide repertoire of strategies for solving problems, which includes knowing when to add, subtract, multiply, and divide, but also includes strategies such as

- looking for patterns
- making tables or lists to organize data
- drawing pictures and diagrams
- guessing, testing, and revising
- working backward
- using logical reasoning.

These strategies give students options for simplifying and solving math problems. But we cannot just tell students how to solve problems; that does not work. Providing focused tasks, guided questions, and opportunities to explore, model, and talk about varied problems is the key. When students have knowledge of a wide array of possible strategies, they are able to select ones that work for the given problem.

Strategies are not learned all at once or at one grade level; they are learned over time as they are applied to different content and are extended and refined throughout the elementary years (NCTM 2000). A critical way to build students' repertoire of strategies is having students share and justify their methods. Tasks that have one solution but multiple ways to get to the solution (as in Figure 1.12) provide opportunities for students to discuss their varied approaches and make sense of the different strategies they use (Spangler et al. 2014).

Problem: Bailey made 1 gallon of lemonade for her lemonade stand. She sold $\frac{3}{4}$ gallon of the lemonade on Monday. On Tuesday, she sold $\frac{1}{2}$ of what was left. How much did she sell on Tuesday?

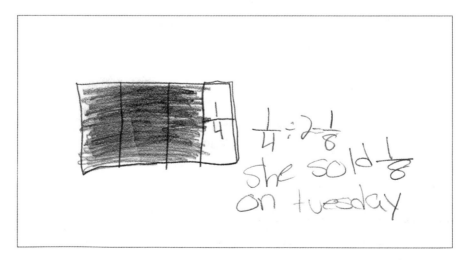

Figure 1.12

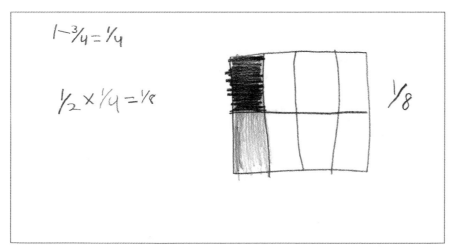

Figure 1.12 Both students use diagrams to visualize the problem. For the second step, one chooses to divide the remaining $\frac{1}{4}$ gallon by 2 and the other multiplies it by $\frac{1}{2}$, stimulating productive classroom discussions about their problem-solving decisions, the operations they use, and the connections between division and fractions.

Tips for Helping Students Choose a Strategy

Pinch Cards

Provide repeated practice selecting operations with quick but thoughtful pinch card discussions. Give each student a pinch card (see Figure 1.13) and pose a math word problem to the class. Students then:

1. silently pinch the sign that shows the operation they would use to solve the problem, showing the teacher
2. turn to a partner and share the operation they would use to solve the problem, justifying why they chose that operation
3. share their ideas with the class about which operation makes sense for the problem and, together with the teacher, build the equation to match the problem situation.

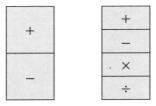

Figure 1.13 Pinch cards for primary grades show addition and subtraction, and those for intermediate grades show all four operations. All students are actively involved in thinking about operations as they select and pinch the operation they hear reflected in the problem context.

continues

Pinch cards offer a quick check for understanding as the teacher is able to see the operations selected by each student. Having students justify why they chose the operation is an integral part of the activity, allowing them opportunities to share their thinking with both partners and the class. It engages all students in thinking about the operations and prompts classroom discussions focusing on why specific operations make sense for specific problems.

Problem-Solving Strategies List

As strategies are introduced and discussed in class, record them on a class chart, as in Figure 1.14. This list of possible problem-solving strategies becomes a reference for students during problem-solving tasks. Following tasks, have students share the strategy they selected and justify why it made sense for that problem.

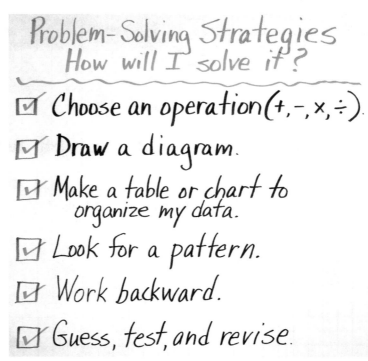

Figure 1.14 Each class' strategies list will look a bit different because the lists are compiled based on the strategies the class has discussed during their problem-solving investigations.

DEVELOPING A PROBLEM-SOLVING DISPOSITION

As important as it is for our students to know and apply a variety of problem-solving strategies, knowing strategies is not enough. Believing you can solve a problem, being willing to take a risk and try a strategy, and having the perseverance to stick with the task are critical qualities of effective problem solvers.

Effective problem solvers:

- believe they can solve problems; they are confident
- take risks; they act on hunches and are sometime wrong, but learn from their mistakes
- keep trying, even when the method or solution is not readily apparent
- reflect on their actions, make adjustments, and keep working toward solutions
- are patient, knowing that some problems take time to solve.

Problem solvers recognize that confusion is a part of solving problems and discover that persistence pays off.

Helping students develop a problem-solving disposition is as important as helping them acquire computational and procedural skills. We play a critical role in developing these dispositions by setting up K–5 classrooms that offer opportunities for students to explore cognitively demanding tasks in safe environments in which risk taking and patience are valued. By establishing a classroom climate that nurtures reflection and risk taking, accepts that students get stuck, encourages them to find ways to get unstuck, allows questioning of each other's methods, and acknowledges that learning arises from failures as well as successes (NCTM 2000), we are creating an environment in which problem solvers thrive.

The ability to persevere is vital to developing a problem-solving disposition, but there are many reasons students may not persevere as much as we would like them to. Students may give up for any of the following reasons:

- They don't have the skills they need to succeed at a particular task.
- They *think* they can't succeed.
- They are faced with a complex problem of a type they do not have experience with.
- They lack experience persevering, or don't know what to do to get unstuck.
- They don't believe that perseverance is valued.

Let's look at each of these situations and some ways we can help students deal with them.

Students give up when they don't have the skills to succeed.

Many of our students are right in feeling that they can't solve a problem because they lack the skills to do it. As we help them find ways to comprehend, visualize, and solve problems we are both arming them with the skills they need and building their confidence with problem-solving tasks.

But some students may be at different levels. A problem may be just right for one team, but at a frustration level for another. Consider differentiating problem tasks to allow all students to find success (see more in Chapter 5). Although all of the following problems require students to use their understanding of money, the data allow for different levels of skill.

- Colleen had 2 dimes, 5 nickels, and 15 pennies. How much money did she have?
- Colleen had 3 quarters, 2 dimes, 5 nickels, and 15 pennies. How much money did she have?
- Colleen had just the right amount of money to buy a granola bar for $1.25. What coins could she have used?

Students give up when they think they can't succeed.

A focus on the right answer causes many students to become immediately anxious when a problem-solving task is posed. Whether they have the skills or not, many of them believe they can't succeed.

- Do students feel safe to try, even if they can't find the answer?
- Does their anxiety stop them from moving through the task?
- Will building their confidence help them take risks?

As we create an environment in which process and effort are valued, students begin to relax and gain confidence. Consider the following to alleviate anxiety during problem-solving tasks:

- Focus on the process, not the answer. Spend more time discussing their thinking strategies than answers. Focus discussions on their methods and reasoning. Show students that you value the how and why of their problem-solving experiences more than the answer.
- Have students turn and share strategies with partners to allow them to discuss and process their ideas. Quick turn-and-share activities can jump-start reluctant students.
- Acknowledge and verbalize the complexity of some tasks. Let students know that everyone gets confused with some problems, including you! Acknowledge that confusion is part of being a problem solver, but that good problem solvers find ways to move through the confusion (e.g., visualizing the problem, talking with a partner, thinking about related problems).
- Have students solve problems with partners or teams. Not only does this allow them to process their ideas and gain new perspectives from others, but it offers the solidarity of finding a solution together, relieving the anxiety of being on one's own. And in the process, students are hearing others' thinking and seeing what it looks like to think like a problem solver.
- Have a class time-out as needed to refocus students on the task and decrease stress. As some students share tips and suggestions, others gain new direction or insights to be able to persevere through the task.
- Debrief after problem tasks to highlight methods. As students share varied methods, they recognize that problems do not have to be solved in one way; there are options for finding solutions. As students hear alternate methods, they build a greater repertoire of strategies and gain confidence for future tasks.

Students give up when faced with more complex problems if they lack experience with those types of problems.

Students need experience exercising perseverance. If all of the tasks they are posed are simple and brief, they aren't challenged to develop the skill to hang in with more complex tasks. Classroom experiences in which students explore and discuss two-step or multistep problems are vital. Discussing varied ways to find solutions for open middle problems (problems with one answer but multiple ways to get there) helps students see there is not just one path to the solution. And posing rich problems that have more than one answer, like the following, provides practice persevering to find those multiple solutions:

- If 10 children were at the party, how many were boys and how many were girls?
- How could Aidan pay for a cupcake that costs 35 cents, using exact change? Prove that each combination of coins equals 35 cents.
- What are some different rectangles that can be formed with 36 square tiles? What are their dimensions?
- Charlie had a string of licorice that was 26 inches long. He cut it into 3 pieces. How long could each of the pieces have been?
- 2 children shared a pizza. When they were done eating, $\frac{1}{6}$ of the pizza was left. What fraction of the pizza could each child have eaten?
- Mr. Short had 38 feet of fencing to build a pen for the dog. What could the area of the pen have been? Draw diagrams to justify your answers.

Students give up when they don't understand what it means to persevere or what to do when they get stuck.

Have a class discussion about perseverance. Create a class definition for the word (e.g., "We don't give up when it gets hard. We look for another way to find the answer."). Acknowledge that getting stuck is part of being a problem solver, but that good problem solvers find ways to get unstuck. Have students work in teams to come up with ideas for what they could do if they get stuck solving a problem. Create a chart to display their ideas and post it in the room for reference. The ideas might include:

- Use materials to model the problem.
- Draw a diagram of the problem.
- Reread the problem to remember what we were trying to solve.
- Think of another problem that is like that one and think about how we solved that problem.
- Make the data simpler.
- Think about the problem with no data at all.
- Ask a friend for an idea.

Frequently ask students if they got stuck during the problem-solving task, and if so, to share how they got unstuck.

Students give up when they don't understand that perseverance is valued.

Praise effort and perseverance, not just right answers. Be specific in your praise so students understand what you value. Through specific comments, they gain a better perspective of what it means to persevere (see Figure 1.15).

> *That wasn't what you were thinking in the beginning, was it? I like the way you changed your mind after you noticed . . .*

You did a great job adjusting your approach! When you realized you couldn't fold the paper any more, you recorded the data instead of giving up and it led you to the answer!

Let students know that perseverance is valued in your classroom.

Figure 1.15 Through our comments and feedback, we show students that we value their effort and perseverance as they face the challenge of complex math tasks.

Conclusion

Mathematicians are thinkers. As we explore instructional strategies throughout this book, you will notice how the problems we pose, the questions we ask, the tools we choose, and the talk we generate lead our students to insights and understanding and create a positive and energizing classroom climate in which our students develop as mathematical thinkers. And our students' thinking is deepened when we make connections between the skills they are learning and connect math to their lives. We explore the importance of these connections in Chapter 2.

 Scan this QR code or visit http://hein.pub/MathinPractice to see videos related to inquiry and questioning and to access additional online resources (use keycode MIPGT).

Study Group Questions

1. What math concepts lend themselves to discovery lessons?
2. How might you set up an investigation for students to discover a math idea? What data would students gather and observe? What questions might you ask?
3. How do your questions impact the level of thinking done by students?
4. In what ways might your comments to students' responses impact a class discussion?
5. How can you help students comprehend problems?
6. What does perseverance look like in a math classroom? Why is it important for your students to develop perseverance?
7. In what ways can you build your students' perseverance?

Build Bridges, Make Connections

Connecting Math Concepts to Each Other and to Our Students' Lives

In our effort to create classrooms in which math makes sense to our students, making connections is vital. Learning is about making sense of new ideas by connecting them to prior knowledge. By making connections to what our students already know, we are able to help them gain new insights. Making connections between math ideas (e.g., fractions and measurement) deepens our students' understanding as they discover common threads between various math topics. And making connections between math and our students' lives allows them to think about math as real and meaningful to them.

We strive to help our students use the interconnectedness of mathematics to better understand its skills and concepts. We look for big ideas that span the K–5 years, connections between the math topics we introduce, and skill progressions from simple to more complex to capitalize on what our students already know and help them make sense of new ideas. Math skills and concepts progress gradually over the years. Our curriculum, through the use of progressions, gently adds new knowledge and skills, relying on the foundations built in previous years. Students' mastery of a skill at one level allows them to understand and refine that skill at a deeper level.

A significant factor in the development of students' understanding of mathematics is their recognition of when and how math is used in the world around them. We know the excitement and energy that results when what we are teaching strikes a chord in our students' lives. And these real-world connections help them make sense of the abstract nature of mathematics and find meaning in its numbers, symbols, properties, and rules. By placing math skills in a problem context, using real data during math investigations, and showing math contexts through events in children's literature, our students experience mathematics as connected to their lives.

What the Research, Standards, and Experts Say About Making Connections

NCTM (2000) contends that math learning is deepened when students connect math ideas within the study of mathematics as well as to their own lives. Connections help students see mathematics as an integrated whole rather than a set of separate skills and concepts and, as students see math ideas build from one level to the next, they see the structure of math. The Common Core State Standards (National Governors Association Center for Best Practices and Council of Chief State School Officers 2010) expands on that idea to maintain that students who are mathematically proficient see and use the structure of math as they explore and make sense of math ideas. In their Standard for Mathematical Practice #7, they emphasize the importance of students seeing the big ideas that lie beneath the many skills and concepts, acknowledging their connections to each other.

Conceptual understanding is developmental; we build on knowledge by linking new concepts to existing knowledge. Fosnot and Jacob (2010) encourage teaching practices that build connections between math ideas so students view math as a discipline of interconnected topics and concepts.

In *Principles to Actions*, the NCTM highlights connections in its Mathematics Teaching Practices through Practice #1: Establish mathematics goals to focus learning. As teachers plan for math instruction, it is suggested that they consider the goals for student learning and think about those goals in a progression to effectively determine a starting point and decide on ways to connect the new ideas to previous learning (NCTM 2014).

Making Connections Between and Among Math Ideas

Making connections between previous and new learning and among varied math topics helps our students better understand the ideas of math. By beginning with what is known and building from there, students make sense of math a little at a time. And by highlighting connections between various math topics, they begin to better see math as a connected discipline. As we plan math lessons, making connections should be a primary consideration.

- What are our learning goals?
- What have students already learned about this skill/concept?
- What other math topics have we discussed that connect to this?
- How can we make connections between what they know and the new ideas that will be explored?
- For what upcoming skills/concepts are we providing a foundation?

Our goal is to help our students build gradual understanding by making explicit connections to previous learning and to related math concepts.

BUILDING GRADUAL UNDERSTANDING THROUGH PROGRESSIONS

Fundamental learning theories remind us that students learn when new knowledge and skills are connected to previously learned knowledge and skills. A first step to introducing a new skill is looking back on what students know and finding a way to build on that understanding. Understanding the progression of math skills and knowledge is critical for finding the right entry point into a lesson and determining the best questions to ask or investigations to orchestrate.

Luckily for us, math progressions have received a great deal of emphasis in recent years and accessing K–5 progressions is right at our fingertips. The Common Core State Standards developed a detailed progression of math skills. When we determine where our students are in that progression, we are able to decide next steps, building on previous understandings. Consider our students' understanding of fractions.

Grade 1—Students begin to examine the idea of partitioning as they work with rectangles and circles in geometry. They learn the words *halves* and *fourths* and investigate different ways to represent each concept.

Grade 2—Students continue to explore partitioning in geometry, including partitioning into halves, fourths, and thirds. They develop basic understandings about the whole being important and that halves, thirds, or fourths do not have to look the same but must represent equal shares.

Grade 3—Students begin a formal study of fractions and are introduced to a new notation for half ($\frac{1}{2}$), third ($\frac{1}{3}$), and fourth ($\frac{1}{4}$), exploring what numerators and denominators represent. They continue to visualize fractions using geometric shapes but are introduced to other visual models like number lines and set models. They begin to notice that $\frac{4}{4}$ is a whole, that some fractions show the same amount ($\frac{1}{2} = \frac{2}{4}$), and that $\frac{3}{4}$ is the same as 3 one-fourths.

Grade 4—Students extend their understanding of equivalence by discovering ways to generate equivalent fractions. They apply their understanding of addition and subtraction to add fractions with like denominators, building models to visualize the process. They apply their understanding of multiplication to multiply a fraction by a whole number and realize that $4 \times \frac{1}{2}$ is $\frac{1}{2} + \frac{1}{2} + \frac{1}{2} + \frac{1}{2}$.

Grade 5—Students connect their understanding of generating equivalent fractions and their understanding of adding and subtracting fractions with like denominators to add and subtract fractions with unlike denominators. They build on their knowledge of multiplying a fraction by a whole number to multiply a fraction by a fraction, again using models to visualize and connect the process to previous learning. They are introduced to division with a unit fraction and a whole number (e.g., $\frac{1}{2} \div 4$ or $4 \div \frac{1}{2}$) to gain foundational understanding and pave the way for dividing fractions in sixth grade.

With each step of the progression, our students build on their previous understandings and add new learning to their repertoire. They model, discuss, and make connections as they acquire new skills and understandings.

For more detailed information on the progressions in the Common Core State Standards, see the progressions documents at http://math.arizona.edu/~ime/progressions/.

THINKING ABOUT PROGRESSIONS AND CONNECTIONS FOR STANDARD ALGORITHMS

Attention to a progression of skills and making connections between math topics (e.g., place value and addition) help us move students toward procedural fluency. We want our students to be able to efficiently add, subtract, multiply, and divide with whole numbers, fractions, and decimals. In the past, our strategy was to teach the steps to a standard algorithm (as in Figure 2.1) right from the start.

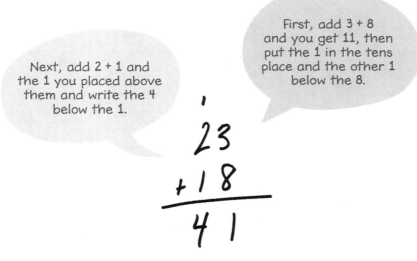

Figure 2.1

Did we ever talk about the numbers we were adding: 23 and 18? Did students even think about what a reasonable sum might be? Did they know why a 1 was placed above the 2?

When executed correctly, these traditional algorithms get us to the right answer every time. But do they make sense? Do students understand the process? Standard algorithms involve performing a series of steps focused on digits, not numbers. When we skip the process of visualizing and discussing the math connected to these steps, our students' understanding of numbers and operations suffers. We notice that they make errors, missing steps because they have memorized the steps rather than understood them. Students get unreasonable answers because they are focused on digits and procedures rather than thinking about the numbers. In math, we value efficiency, but we also value understanding.

- What prior understandings will help students make sense of these procedures?
- What experiences with strategies based on place value understandings and properties will build their understanding?
- How will making connections between these place value strategies and the efficient steps of the standard algorithm create the needed bridge to produce both understanding and efficiency?

The foundation for standard algorithms begins early. Kindergarten students compose numbers to make 10. They learn what it means to add. As students begin to explore place value, they identify the difference between the value of the digits in the tens and ones places. As they add 2-digit numbers, a critical understanding is that tens are added to tens and ones are added to ones, and when it is needed we can make a 10 from 10 ones. These place value understandings arm students with a foundational understanding of how our number system is organized.

Why not think about 23 + 18 as it connects to students' prior knowledge about addition and place value? About what might our answer be? How do you know? Could we combine the tens and combine the ones to find the sum? How many tens will we have when they are combined and how many ones? Can we visualize this with a model (see Figure 2.2)?

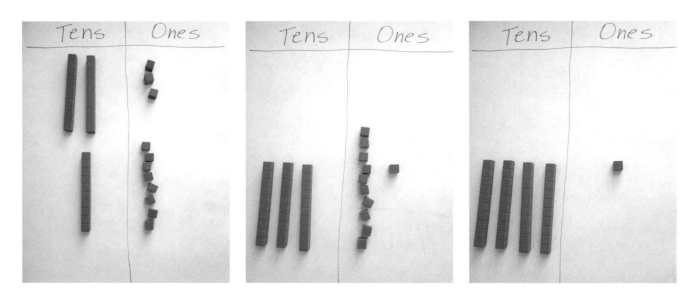

23 + 18 = __

Figure 2.2 Students visualize the addition with base-ten blocks and use their prior place value understanding to find the sum.

First, students model each number with base-ten blocks showing their place value understanding. Then, they use their understanding of addition to combine tens and then ones, finding that 2 tens + 1 ten = 3 tens and 3 ones + 8 ones = 11 ones. But wait, that's too many ones! Now, they think back on their experiences renaming numbers—what number is 3 tens and 11 ones? This important previously learned place value concept provides needed understanding here.

Or students might visualize this on a number line to see that 23 + 10 is 33 and 33 + 7 = 40 and 40 + 1 = 41. As they think about it in this way, they are capitalizing on their understanding of addition as adding to and revisiting their place value skills as they break apart numbers to model the process on a number line as in Figure 2.3.

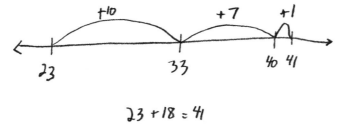

Figure 2.3 Students are able to visualize addition using open number lines and practice breaking numbers apart to make the addition process simpler. This student first adds 10, then adds 7 to get to 40, and then adds the 1 more.

Students transition from using these visual strategies to performing the computations with numbers only, using their understanding of expanded form to decompose the numbers, add them by place value, and then add the partial sums to find their answer as in Figure 2.4. They use their concrete and visual experiences to better understand this more symbolic approach.

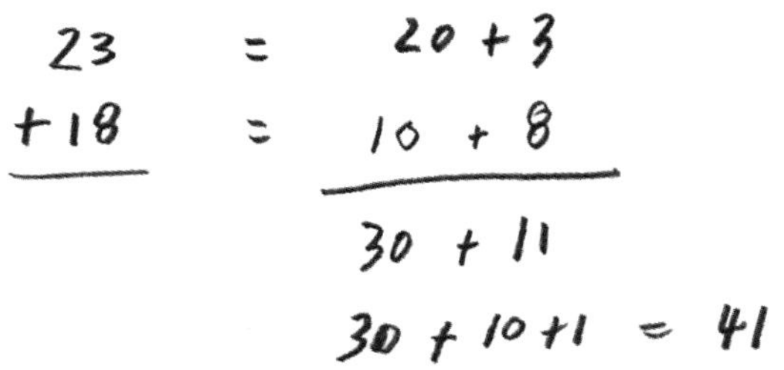

$$
\begin{array}{rcl}
23 & = & 20 + 3 \\
+18 & = & 10 + 8 \\
\hline
& & 30 + 11 \\
& & 30 + 10 + 1 = 41
\end{array}
$$

Figure 2.4 Students build on the foundations of their hands-on and visual models to represent the addition process using numbers and symbols.

The goal is not that students always use base-ten blocks or number lines or expanded form to solve 2-digit addition problems. In fact, they will most likely use the standard algorithm that we teach them by making connections to these place value strategies. But without these prior experiences with models and discussions, they miss the opportunity to build a strong understanding of numbers and operations and to have the foundations to understand the standard algorithm. We follow a progression beginning with foundational number and place value skills, then visualizing the process with models, and then transitioning students to a number-based approach and then to the standard algorithm. We no longer rush to the standard algorithm. Today, we use our time wisely to lead them to the algorithm through a series of foundational progressions.

Tips for Utilizing Progressions

Know the Before and After

The more we know about the development of a skill or concept during the prior year, the better we are able to find just the right starting point as we add complexity to that skill or concept. And taking a look to see what will be introduced the following year is critical so we are able to provide a strong foundation for what is coming next. Although a second-grade teacher may not immediately see the need to explore arrays and area models with repeated addition equations (see Figure 2.5), exposure to these models reaps great benefits as students explore them in their introduction to multiplication the following year.

In each Math in Practice grade-level book, learning progressions show how skills and concepts develop from the previous grade to the following grade.

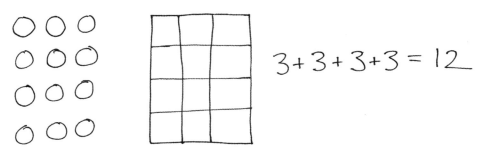

Figure 2.5 Students see the array or area model as showing 4 rows of 3 or 3 + 3 + 3 + 3 = 12 in second grade and revisit the familiar models as 4 rows of 3 or 4 × 3 = 12 in third grade, giving meaning to the often memorized "multiplication is repeated addition."

Vertical Discussions

There is great value to discussions between teachers at the same grade level, as we plan collaboratively, share strategies, develop common assessments, or discuss the intricacies of meeting our students' needs, but there are added benefits to discussions with those teaching the grade level before and after us. Hearing what skills may be weak for students who enter the following grade helps us focus our efforts to provide them with the foundations they will need. Sharing our strategies, approaches, models, or even vocabulary with their new teachers helps ensure that connections can be made to our students' previous experiences as their new teacher attempts to build on the foundation we have provided. And that same information from their previous teacher allows us to know the appropriate starting point as we begin a new year by making connections to their past experiences.

A Focus on Big Ideas

Our focus at each grade level is on the major standards addressed at that level, but as we look more closely, we notice ideas that weave through that major work across K–5. Some important ideas that are revisited across grade levels include:

- understanding that numbers are flexible (can be decomposed and composed)
- understanding the role of patterns in our number system
- understanding how place value works
- understanding operations on numbers
- understanding equality and inequality
- understanding properties of operations
- understanding the relationship between parts and whole.

Big ideas !

In each of these cases, the concepts first appear in primary grades and are revisited and refined across the K–5 years.

Most of us spent little classroom time talking about the big ideas of math. Our brains were filled with lots of rules and what seemed to us to be unrelated bits of information, and little time was spent talking about the big ideas that held all of these skills together. Our goal for today's elementary math students is that they develop an understanding of the big ideas of math, that they understand how math works. To achieve this, we must make sure that our lessons are solidly grounded in and directed toward big math ideas, rather than lessons that focus only on the mechanics of math processes. Rather than memorizing the definition of the distributive property, we focus on the flexibility of numbers and how they can be broken apart or put together to make computations more efficient. Instead of the mechanics of constructing line plots or bar graphs, we focus on the ways we can display data to help us organize and visualize information so we can more easily draw conclusions from it. Instead of focusing on the mechanics of addition with decimals, we focus on the connections to addition with whole numbers including when we add, how we do it, and how we know that our answer makes sense. We help students grasp the big picture so they are able to see beyond each specific skill to understand the big ideas that make it work.

HIGHLIGHTING BIG IDEAS

Big ideas highlight what is important and consistent about math. They are the link that ties the small stuff together and helps it make sense. They represent the structure of math.

So, how do we focus on big ideas? A good example of a shift in focus is evident as we look at how we teach basic math facts today as compared to how we were taught them. In the past, we focused on the facts themselves and memorized them so we knew them by memory and could use them when doing computations. Although we still want our students to know their math facts, today we see the importance of uncovering the big ideas that build the foundation for how these facts work. As we plan to teach math facts, we consider some pretty important math understandings:

- Do students understand properties? How would an understanding of the commutative or distributive properties impact their understanding of math facts?
- Do they understand equality? What does it mean to say 3 + 4 is equal to 7? Is it true that 3 × 4 = 2 × 6? Why?
- What does it mean to add, subtract, multiply, or divide? What do the symbols (+, −, ×, ÷) imply about what the answer might look like?
- How are addition and subtraction related? How are multiplication and division related? Would knowing 4 × 5 = 20 help them know and understand 20 ÷ 5?
- Can numbers be missing in any place in an equation? How would I know what belongs in the blank for 10 + __ = 15 or __ × 3 = 21? How does that connect to 15 − 10 or 21 ÷ 3?

Although knowing the facts themselves is important and supports our students' computational fluency, how much more would students gain if the facts were taught through models, discussions, and investigations that lead to insights about these big ideas? When these ideas are made explicit, our students reap the benefit of deeper understanding that is transferrable to many math situations. Rather than memorizing 24 ÷ 8 = 3, our students immediately know that this is the same as __ × 8 = 24. They know why 24 = 8 × 3 is true, regardless of where the equal sign is located, and that 8 × 3 = 3 × 8. And by investigating and discussing these ideas with each successive fact set, they revisit them and develop a deep understanding that these recurrent ideas transcend one situation or skill.

Note that in the grade-level books, you will find many of these
big ideas highlighted during math facts lessons.

BIG IDEAS ACROSS THE YEARS

Big ideas are central to understanding math and are woven across varied grade levels. As an example, consider the idea that numbers are flexible—they can be put together (composed) and taken apart (decomposed) in varied ways without changing their value (see Figure 2.6).

How might this big idea appear at varied grade levels?

Kindergarten

5 can be decomposed in different ways: 5 = 3 + 2 or 5 = 4 + 1.
Teen numbers represent 10 and some more; 13 is 10 and 3 more.

Grade 1

Numbers can be decomposed in varied ways. 24 = 2 tens and 4 ones, but also 1 ten and 14 ones.
We can decompose numbers to add. We know that 24 + 20 = 44 because 2 tens + 2 tens = 4 tens, and 4 tens + 4 ones = 44.
We can solve the math fact 6 + 5 = 11 because 6 + 4 = 10, so if we decompose 5 into 4 + 1 we know 6 + 5 is 1 more than 6 + 4.

Figure 2.6 Students begin exploring how numbers can be decomposed in kindergarten and then build upon the idea throughout the elementary years.

Grade 2

We continue to decompose numbers to add. 25 + 38 = 20 + 30 and 5 + 8; 50 + 13 = 63 (we can compose a 10 from 13 because it is 10 + 3).

When subtracting 47 − 19, we rename 47. We think of it as 3 tens and 17 ones, then we can subtract 1 ten and 9 ones.

Grade 3

We continue to compose and decompose numbers as we explore addition and subtraction with multidigit numbers.

We think about decomposing $\frac{3}{4}$ into 3 one-fourths.

Grade 4

We decompose fractions to find that $\frac{5}{8} = \frac{1}{8} + \frac{1}{8} + \frac{3}{8}$, but $\frac{5}{8}$ also equals $\frac{4}{8} + \frac{1}{8}$.

We split decimals into tenths and hundredths, knowing 0.56 = 0.5 + 0.06.

We express numbers in expanded form and use partial products to find the products of multi-digit factors.

We think of division as breaking apart numbers to find partial quotients.

Grade 5

We decompose numbers in expanded form and by thinking of powers of 10; 3×10^3 is $3 \times 10 \times 10 \times 10$ or 3×1000.

This big idea, that numbers can be composed and decomposed but retain their value, appears across the K–5 spectrum. With each year that it is revisited, in a new and more complex way, our students gain a deeper understanding of numbers. Our goal is to help them look beyond simply identifying tens and ones or using expanded form to see the big picture of how numbers work. Our goal is to help them connect the skills across the years to discover the big ideas. We ask questions like:

> *What does this remind you of?*
> *Where have we seen this before?*
> *How is this like . . . ?*

Good Picture,
"Big Picture"
Big Idea
Big Idea
Questions.

To highlight and uncover these recurring ideas, we ask our students to visualize math to discover patterns and repetition (Chapter 3), to talk about the math they are doing (Chapter 4), and to make connections between math skills. We help them see beyond the specific to the big ideas.

Making Sense of Math Through Real Contexts

It is important for our students to make connections between math skills. Through these connections they view math as a connected discipline and are able to build new learning from previous learning. They are able to discern big ideas that permeate the math curriculum and see those ideas as they are extended and expanded. But it is also critical for our math students to see connections between mathematics and their lives. Through problem contexts, the use of real data, and scenarios from children's literature, our students begin to see math as making sense in the world.

PROBLEMS GIVE MATH MEANING

When was the last time someone handed you an equation to solve just for the sake of solving it? In fact, other than in math class, performing math computations out of context is quite unusual. Word problems give a context to $3 + 5$ or $\frac{1}{2} \times 6$.

> 3 cherry lollipops and 5 lemon lollipops becomes $3 + 5 =$ ___.
> Allison's 6 pencils, $\frac{1}{2}$ of which are sharpened, becomes $\frac{1}{2} \times 6 = n$.

Through problems, the numbers and symbols have meaning. Problems also allow students to see situations in which they need to find a perimeter, convert measurements, determine elapsed time, compare monetary amounts, or combine measurements. Rather than being classroom exercises, problems show a purpose to learning math skills.

PROBLEMS PROVIDE A CONTEXT FOR UNDERSTANDING MATH OPERATIONS

A central understanding in mathematics is the understanding of math operations. What is the purpose of our students learning how to subtract $65 - 34$ if they don't understand what the expression means? Students learn about the operation of subtraction by examining contexts for $65 - 34$ like:

- Mrs. King baked 65 cookies. She sent 34 to school for her son's class. How many cookies did she have left? (taking from)
- There were 65 second graders. 34 were girls. How many were boys? (separating/taking apart)
- Caroline sold 65 boxes of cookies and Aidan sold 34 boxes. How many more boxes did Caroline sell? (comparing)

Without the problem contexts, $65 - 34$ is simply an expression. With the contexts, students see three different structures that show subtraction. That same expression might represent taking from, taking apart, or comparing. Rather than focusing solely on *how* to subtract, the problems allow students to gain a deep understanding of *when* to subtract.

Building an Understanding of Operations Through Problems

From their earliest experiences, our students learn about the meaning of operations through problems. The stories, or situations, reveal repetitive structures that bring meaning to each operation. Students begin to recognize situations that indicate addition, subtraction, multiplication, or division. They develop an understanding of the action or relationship represented by each operation. The abstract symbols $(+, -, \times, \div)$ begin to take on meaning.

> There were 4 dogs in the park.
> 1 more dog came.
> How many dogs were in the park?

There are some dogs and another dog joins them. We are adding: $4 + 1 = 5$.

> There were 4 dogs in the park.
> 1 ran home.
> How many dogs were in the park?

There were 4, but 1 ran away. We are subtracting: $4 - 1 = 3$.

Consider the sample problems in Figure 2.7 that illustrate the structures for addition, subtraction, multiplication, and division.

Operation	Problem Examples	Story Structures
Addition	Bailey had 6 pennies in her pocket. She found 3 more pennies. How many pennies did she have? $6 + 3 = 9$	Adding to
	There were 6 red apples and 4 yellow apples in the bowl. How many apples were in the bowl? $6 + 4 = 10$	Putting together
Subtraction	Blake had 6 balloons. 2 of them popped. How many were left? $6 - 2 = 4$	Taking from
	There were 26 children in Mrs. Bingham's class. 14 were boys. How many were girls? $26 - 14 = 12$	Taking apart/separating
	Molly is 42 inches tall. Kellen is 38 inches tall. How much taller is Molly?	Comparing
Multiplication	Katie had 3 vases with 6 flowers in each vase. How many flowers did she have? $3 \times 6 = 18$	Combining equal groups
	Liam ran 2 miles. Colin ran 3 times as far as Liam. How far did Colin run? $3 \times 2 = 6$	Comparing based on how many times more (multiplicative comparison)
Division	There were 35 children on the playground. The teacher split them into teams of 5. How many teams were there? $35 \div 5 = 7$	Splitting into equal groups (number of groups unknown)
	There were 35 children on the playground. The teacher split them into 7 teams. How many people were on each team? $35 \div 7 = 5$	Splitting into equal groups (number in each group unknown)
	The tree was 20 feet tall. It was 5 times as tall as the bush. How tall was the bush?	Division based on comparison

Figure 2.7 When students think about the action or relationship in the problem they are able to identify the operation that fits the problem.

As students hear problems, retell and model the problems, recognize the story structure, and associate it with an operation, they are making important connections between real situations and abstract representations.

See more in the grade-level books on understanding story structures.

Understanding Unknowns Through Problem Contexts

A challenge for many students is making sense of equations in which unknowns are in different positions (e.g., $12 + \underline{} = 28$ or $3 \times \underline{} = 45$). Now, instead of simply looking for the sum or product, an addend or factor is missing from the problem. In a *put together* problem, we don't know one part, but we do know the whole. In an *adding to* problem, we may not know how much is added to the start amount or we may not know the start amount. Without word problems to illustrate $12 + \underline{} = 28$, it feels confusing and abstract, but connecting the equation to a problem situation makes it understandable.

- Mrs. Alexander baked 12 sugar cookies and some peanut butter cookies. She baked 28 cookies altogether. How many peanut butter cookies did she bake?
- Jacqui had 3 identical sheets of stickers and had 45 stickers altogether. How many stickers were on each sheet?

Along with illustrating the missing addend or missing factor equations, the problem contexts promote discussions about inverse operations. We said $3 \times \underline{} = 45$, but couldn't we have also said $45 \div 3 = \underline{}$? Word problems allow students to see and explore abstract math concepts through their contexts.

Certainly we want our students to be able to find the answer for $13 + 5 = \underline{}$ or $\frac{1}{2} \times 4 = n$, but our hope is that they understand math skills and processes deeply enough to know when to apply them in real situations. In life, they will not be filling in worksheets, but will face situations in which they must apply what they know about math. Classroom experiences must balance the teaching of *how* to perform the computation with the knowledge of *when* to perform the computation. Integrating problems into our lessons on a daily basis, and discussing the operation associated with each problem, helps us achieve this balance.

Moving Between Real (Context) and Abstract (Equations)

For many students, a particularly difficult part of the problem-solving process is building the appropriate equation to match the problem. (This relates to comprehending the problem, which we discussed in Chapter 1.) The numbers and symbols in the equation should match the events and data in the story problem, and yet those connections elude many students who resort to plucking numbers from the problem, adding an operation sign, and hoping for the best (see Figure 2.8). Although this student may know how to find the answer to $21 \div 7 = n$ when given the equation, she was unable to build the equation from the problem context.

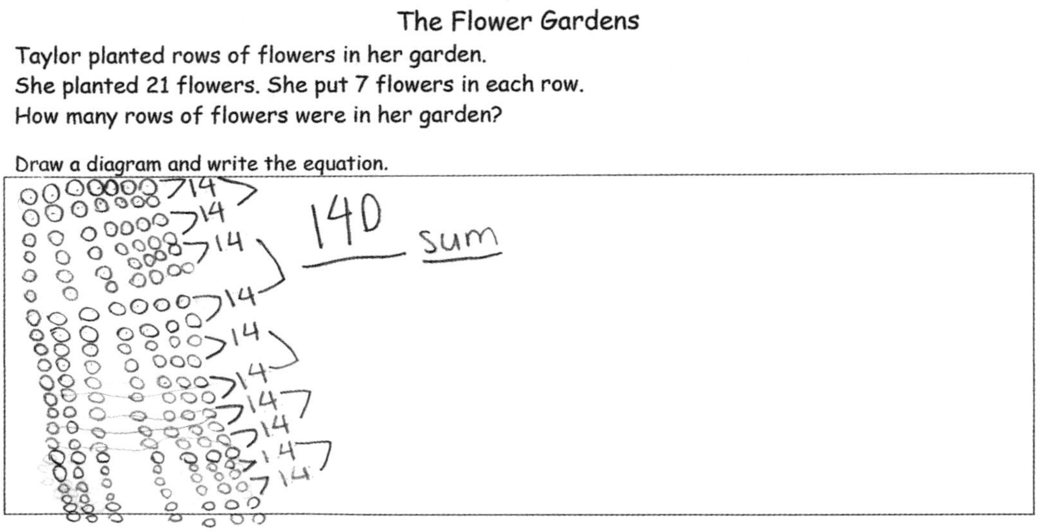

The Flower Gardens

Taylor planted rows of flowers in her garden.
She planted 21 flowers. She put 7 flowers in each row.
How many rows of flowers were in her garden?

Draw a diagram and write the equation.

Figure 2.8 This student sees 21 and 7 in the problem and draws 21 rows of 7, then incorrectly finds the sum, yet the problem was about 21 flowers with 7 in each row. Her answer is 140, which represents the number of rows of flowers in the garden, making no sense because there were only 21 flowers.

Standard 2 in the Common Core Standards for Mathematical Practice highlights the importance of our students' abilities to decontextualize and contextualize. When faced with a problem situation, our students are challenged to decontextualize (remove the context and replace it with an abstract representation, an equation, that reflects the situation). When students build equations, they are decontextualizing.

This ability to move from real to abstract is challenging for students who have not consistently experienced math through problems. Beginning daily lessons with a math problem and guiding students as they express the situation in an abstract way (equation) gives them ongoing practice decontextualizing and deepens their understanding of math equations.

Consider this example:

At the beginning of math class, Mrs. Newell posed the following problem to begin a lesson on multiplying a whole number by a fraction:

> Joe, Kevin, Colleen, and Megan were in a relay race. Each of them ran $\frac{1}{3}$ mile. What was the total distance of the race?

Mrs. Newell asked her students to discuss the problem with their partners.

What are we trying to find out? (How far they all ran together. *Or,* The total distance of the race.)

What data do we need to solve this? (We need to know how far each of them ran and how many people ran.)

Solve the problem with a partner and be ready to share with us.

Which operation would you use? Why? (Addition, because we are looking for a total and when you add you are putting things together to get a total.)

What equation would match this problem? ($\frac{1}{3} + \frac{1}{3} + \frac{1}{3} + \frac{1}{3} = n$ because they all ran $\frac{1}{3}$ mile and there are 4 of them.)

Tell me about the numbers in your equation. What do they represent? (There is a $\frac{1}{3}$ for each person so there are 4 one-thirds because Joe, Kevin, Colleen, and Megan each ran $\frac{1}{3}$ mile. The n is how far they ran together since we added them all up.)

Is there another operation we might have chosen to find the total miles they ran? (Multiplication, because we are looking for a total and you can get that when you multiply, and each of them ran the same amount so you can multiply.)

What multiplication equation would match this problem? (They each ran $\frac{1}{3}$ mile and there were 4 of them so $4 \times \frac{1}{3} = n$.)

Tell me about the numbers in your equation. What do they represent? (The 4 is for the 4 people who ran and the $\frac{1}{3}$ is how far they each ran. The n is how far they ran altogether, but we don't know that.)

Turn to your partner, do you agree or disagree that $\frac{1}{3} + \frac{1}{3} + \frac{1}{3} + \frac{1}{3} = 4 \times \frac{1}{3}$? (Agree because you added 4 one-thirds, but $4 \times \frac{1}{3}$ means 4 one-thirds, too.)

The context of the problem allowed these students to make sense of the multiplication equation. As students move through the remainder of the lesson about multiplying a whole number by a fraction, exploring $3 \times \frac{1}{2}$ or $5 \times \frac{1}{4}$, they have a context to help them make sense of the notation and recognize its connection to repeated addition. Being able to move from a real context to an abstract representation should be an ongoing part of our students' math experiences.

Although solving problems is a great way for students to practice decontextualizing, they also benefit from opportunities to contextualize, to decide on a context for an equation or expression. By posing an equation and having students write a problem to show a possible context, we are challenging them to connect the abstract equation to their understanding of math operations. Consider the examples in Figure 2.9.

By providing opportunities for students to decontextualize and contextualize, we are helping them make connections between real and abstract.

Equation	Possible Context
2 + 3 = __	There were 2 big dogs and 3 little dogs. How many dogs were there?
2 × 5 = n	Carter bought iced tea and lemonade for the class picnic. He bought 5 gallons of each. How many gallons of drinks did he buy for the picnic?
3 × 6 = 18	Anna had 3 sheets of stickers with 6 stickers on each page. How many stickers did she have?
5 × 1.5 = n	Evan bought 5 hamburgers that cost $1.50 each. How much did it cost?

Figure 2.9 Writing their own word problems challenges students to create an appropriate context for the given equation.

Tips for Connecting Problems and Equations

Focus on the Question

In this technique, a set of data is posed at the start of the week. Each day a new problem is posed about the data. Students are asked to talk with partners as in Figure 2.10 and then share with the class their thoughts about the following:

1. *What is the problem about? Retell it in your own words.*
2. *What information is important for solving the problem? Justify the needed information and explain why other posted information is not needed.*
3. *How would you solve the problem? What strategy would you use? What equation would you use and why? Explain your equation.*

This technique focuses on the importance of understanding the problem. It highlights comprehension by asking students to retell the problem, including asking them to identify necessary data and defend their decisions. It also supports students' understanding of the operations as they select and justify which operation makes sense for that day's problem.

Consider the following examples of Focus on the Question tasks:

Example A

Number of Eggs Found During the Egg Hunt

Liam—24

Molly—19

Kellen—37

Bailey—31

Blake—26

1. Liam and Bailey put their eggs in a basket. How many eggs were in the basket? Tell how you would solve it.
2. Blake gave 12 of her eggs to a friend. How many did Blake have left? Tell how you would solve it.
3. How many more eggs did Kellen find than Blake? Tell how you would solve it.
4. Molly's brother gave her 12 more eggs. How many does she have now? Tell how you would solve it.
5. Kellen found 22 pink eggs. The rest of his eggs were blue. How many blue eggs did he find? Tell how you would solve it.

Example B

In the Red Oak School District, there are:

Grade Level	Number of Students
Kindergarten	420
First Grade	426
Second Grade	410
Third Grade	444
Fourth Grade	409
Fifth Grade	385

1. How many chairs will the school district need for the fourth- and fifth-grade students? Tell how you would solve it.
2. How many more desks will the third-grade classes need for their students than the fifth-grade classes will need for their students? Tell how you would solve it.
3. Which two grade levels together have about 850 students? Tell how you would solve it.
4. 796 third- and fourth-grade students attended a winter concert. How many third- and fourth-grade students did not attend the concert? Tell how you would solve it.
5. There were 830 books given away to students at the district's book fair. Each student in kindergarten and one other grade level received a free book. Which other grade level received a free book? Tell how you would solve it.

The set of data remains the same each day, so students must carefully consider each day's question and decide what is being asked, what data are needed based on the question, and what operation makes sense for that day. The answer is deemphasized and discussions revolve around how students would solve the problem. Varied strategies are shared and connections are made between them.

See the online resources and the grade-level books for additional Focus on the Question tasks.

Figure 2.10 These students talk about the data and the problem of the day, deciding how they might solve it.

continues

Pinch Cards

This strategy, shared in Chapter 1, involves all students in thinking about which operation matches the problem situation. Students pinch the operation they would choose, justify why it makes sense with the problem, and discuss how to build the equation to match the problem.

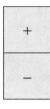 

Writing Word Problems

Students can be asked to work in pairs or teams to write word problems to go along with math equations. Although the stories may be varied, they must make sense with the equation.

23 + 10 = ___

Possible word problem: There were 23 students on the playground. 10 more students joined them. How many students were on the playground?

Another possible problem: Mrs. Morley baked 23 chocolate cupcakes and 10 yellow cupcakes. How many cupcakes did she bake?

Students might be asked to write problems about equations that include operations with whole numbers, fractions, or decimals.

---

*For more on the value of writing word problems
to match equations, see Chapter 4.*

MAKING PROBLEMS REAL

Although all problems offer opportunities for students to engage in the work of being a mathematician, problems that are set in real contexts and connect to the lives of our students allow them to see the usefulness of the math they are learning. Problems that include the names of our students, school, favorite restaurants, or area sports teams engage students and give the math a real and believable setting. Consider posing problems that connect to experiences in your students' lives.

- Derek had $5.65 and Nathan had $7.75. If they put their money together, could they buy a DVD that costs $12.50?
- Mrs. Wallace made toolboxes for students to use during math. She put 4 calculators and 3 rulers in each toolbox. How many calculators and rulers did she need for 8 toolboxes?
- The PE teacher put the 24 students into teams for the day's activity. She wanted the same number of students on each team. How could she have done it?

- The Roosevelt Raiders scored 64 points in Friday's game. Naji scored 16 points to lead the team in scoring. What fraction of the team's points did Naji score?
- Manny's batting average was .312 and Bryce's batting average was .331. Whose batting average was greater? How much greater?

Using real data in the math classroom immediately connects math to real situations. Using sports data from a recent game, admission data to a nearby amusement park, or menu data from a favorite restaurant brings the world into our math classrooms. The newspaper is filled with math data including data from ads, a myriad of statistics on the sports pages, and lots of weather data to compare and analyze. Internet searches yield fun graphs, charts, and tables with real and current data about kids' favorite gifts, the most popular songs, or favorite vacation destinations. Books like *Guinness World Records* (2015), *Time for Kids Almanac* (Time for Kids 2014), *National Geographic Kids Almanac* (National Geographic Kids 2014), and *5000 Awesome Facts (About Everything)!* (National Geographic Kids 2012) are filled with real data that make math fun. Why not compare the weights of the world's largest animals, the heights of the tallest buildings, or the times of the fastest runners? Real data bring energy and authenticity to our math investigations.

USING LITERATURE TO SET A MATH CONTEXT

There is no question that our students love to read and hear stories. Regardless of grade level, they are engaged by the settings, characters, and events (see Figure 2.11). Through listening to and reading stories in which math skills are presented, our students see math in action. Books connect math to the real world.

Figure 2.11 Students become immediately engaged in stories, providing a great opportunity to use the context to explore math concepts.

There is a wealth of children's literature that evokes math themes. Some books are written specifically to teach math skills like the Math Start or Math Matters series, and others are pieces of literature that simply show math in context (e.g., characters joining others show addition in *Rooster's Off to See the World,* or pumpkins rolling off a gate show subtraction in *Five Little Pumpkins*). Kindergarten and first-grade students explore counting in *One Watermelon Seed* or *Ten Apples Up On Top,* and second-grade students investigate number patterns in *Count on Pablo.* Third graders explore fractions in *Full House* and are introduced to division in *The Doorbell Rang.* Fourth-grade students explore characteristics of two-dimensional shapes in *A Cloak for the Dreamer,* and fifth graders reflect on powers of 10 in *On Beyond a Million.* At all levels, there are stories that illustrate the math concepts being introduced and set a context for additional investigations and insights.

See the online resources for a detailed list of children's literature by math topic.

Organizing Literature-Based Lessons

Reading a piece of math-related literature is a great way to begin a math lesson. Students become immediately engaged in the story and a context is set for further explorations and discussions. That context can then be continued throughout the lesson as students discuss, model, and explore the math ideas. To make the most of using children's literature in your math lessons, consider a before-during-after approach.

You will find literature lessons throughout the grade-level books organized in a before-during-after format.

Before Reading

Before-reading activities might activate prior knowledge or assess what students know about the topic. They may develop important vocabulary or background information that helps students better understand the story. They set a purpose for listening to the story, often asking students to listen for specific math connections.

During Reading

During-reading activities are kept to a minimum so students can enjoy the flow of the story. For some books, however, students might be asked to count items on a page, predict the number that will appear when a page is turned, or comment on a shape or fraction represented in an illustration, as the story is being read.

After Reading

After-reading activities focus on students' reflections, interpretations, and extensions of the math ideas. Students might identify the math in the story, use manipulatives to reenact the story, solve problems related to story events, or extend the ideas through investigations. Rather than simply reading a story to the class, using this approach ensures that the story is integrated into the math skill or concept being discussed and that students are actively engaged in problems, discussions, and investigations stimulated by the story context.

Example: Literature as a Context for Learning

Consider the following example:

> Students have been introduced to odd and even numbers through class explorations and now listen to *Even Steven and Odd Todd* by Kathryn Cristaldi and classify numbers related to events in the story by whether they are odd or even.

BEFORE READING:

Briefly introduce the book.

> *Turn and tell your partner what an even number is and what an odd number is.*
> *We are going to read a story about two boys named Even Steven and Odd Todd.*
> *Listen to see if you can figure out why those are their names.*

DURING READING:

Read *Even Steven and Odd Todd.* Pause occasionally to ask students if they notice some reasons behind the boys' names.

AFTER READING:

> *Turn and share: Why are their names Even Steven and Odd Todd?* (Steven does everything with even numbers and Todd does everything with odd numbers.)

Have students fold a paper in half and label one side *Even* and the other side *Odd.*

Have students talk with partners to recall story events (or provide a list on the board: 10 goldfish, 3 knocks at the door, 6 cats, etc.).

> *Which of the events or items go with Even Steven and which go with Odd Todd?*
> *Write each item on the correct side of your paper.*
> *Draw a model for one item on each side of the paper to prove the item is even or odd.*
> *Be ready to explain why each item is placed where it is.*

Have partners share their models and ideas with the class, explaining why each one is either even or odd (see Figure 2.12).

> *With your partner, write one more event for the story. Be sure to show something even and something odd.*

Have partners share their new story events.

Ask the class to agree (thumbs up) or disagree (thumbs down) with their odd and even examples.

Have them complete the following on the back of their paper:

> *An even number is . . .*
> *An odd number is . . .*

Figure 2.12 Students classify story events/items as even or odd and show a model for one item in each category to prove why it is even or odd.

Through Steven and Todd and the silly story events, students became engaged in the topic of odd and even numbers and discussed, modeled, and applied their understanding of the math concept to the story events. The literature made odd and even numbers concrete and fun.

In *Just Enough Carrots* by Stuart J. Murphy, a bunny and his mother shop for food in a grocery store, comparing the quantities they buy to those bought by other shoppers. The concept of same, fewer, and more is illustrated throughout the story. Following the story, students investigate more and fewer with concrete materials, then decide on an item they would like to buy at the grocery store, showing the amount that is the same and an amount that is more and fewer than what they chose to buy (see Figure 2.13).

Figure 2.13 This student chooses 3 bags of crab potato chips, showing 1 bag as fewer than 3 bags and 5 bags as more than 3 bags.

Stories can help students discover patterns in math facts as they see 1 fewer fish on each page in *Ten Sly Piranhas* by William Wise, and then model and discuss the −1 story to discover patterns for −1 facts. Stories can help students visualize the concept of perimeter as they read *Chickens on the Move* by Pam Pollack and Meg Belviso and then solve similar problems about finding possible dimensions for a chicken coop. Or after reading about animal–human comparisons in *If You Hopped like a Frog* by David Schwartz, students might compare numbers of human and animal legs, setting the context for comparing ×2 and ×4 facts. As they explore the number of legs on 3 or 6 or 9 humans and animals, they discuss and discover the relationship between the number patterns that appear.

Through content progressions and connecting new learning to previous ideas, by using problem contexts to connect abstract ideas to real situations, and by capitalizing on the contexts presented through children's literature, we help our students better understand math ideas and see how those ideas connect to their lives. Another key way we help our students understand and make sense of math is through models and representations. By visualizing and manipulating what are often abstract ideas, our students gain insights and build understanding. In the next chapter, we explore the critical role of representations in building that understanding.

 Scan this QR code or visit http://hein.pub/MathinPractice to see videos related to contexts and making connections and to access additional online resources (use keycode MIPGT).

Study Group Questions

1. How might you use your understanding of content progressions to more effectively plan math lessons?
2. What questions might you pose to help students discover connections between various math topics (e.g., linear measurement and fractions)?
3. In what ways can we show students how math connects to their lives?
4. How does the posing of word problems support students' understanding of operations and computations?
5. What real-world data might be integrated into math lessons at your level? How might you integrate these data into your teaching?
6. How do stories (math literature) support math instruction? Share some literature connections you have used with your students.

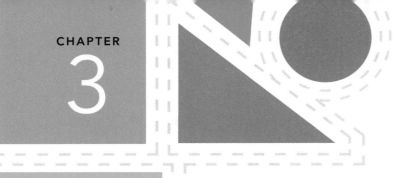

See It, Touch It, Move It

Representations in Math Class

A look into today's elementary math classrooms reveals students exploring math concepts in concrete and visual ways, rather than learning mathematics as abstract ideas. Instead of working solely with numbers, our students represent their math ideas using concrete materials; drawing pictures and diagrams; designing graphs, charts, and tables; and using a variety of symbolic representations. Students see that 6 counters are more than 2 counters, move base-ten blocks to explore the process of subtracting 2-digit numbers, and discover the meaning of equivalent fractions through drawings. Our students create, manipulate, draw, and test varied representations to explore, and ultimately to make sense of, mathematical ideas.

What the Research, Standards and Experts Say About Representations in Math Class

NCTM (2000) recommends that instructional programs enable students to use representations to model math ideas, organize math thinking, communicate math understanding, and solve math problems. In *Principles to Actions*, the NCTM cites "Use and Connect Mathematical Representations" as one of its research-informed Mathematics Teaching Practices that represent "high-leverage practices and essential teaching skills necessary to promote deep learning of mathematics" (NCTM 2014, 9). And the Common Core State Standards for Mathematics (2010) assert that mathematically proficient students model with mathematics and have identified this important practice as one of its Standards for Mathematical Practice.

Our students benefit from opportunities to be actively involved in modeling math ideas, including talking about what they are doing and why they are doing it (National Research Council 2009). Through their interactions with representations, students develop their own understanding of math ideas (Smith 2003). Models help to clarify concepts that are often confused when presented to students solely through abstract (symbolic) representation (Van de Walle and Lovin 2006). Models are not an end in themselves, but a means for our students to construct meaning and communicate understanding (Greeno and Hall 1997).

Providing experiences in which students use varied representations helps them gain deeper understanding of math concepts as they explore and visualize the ideas in varied ways (Goldin 2003; Fuson, Kalchman, and Bransford 2005; Monk and TERC 2003). Students understand math concepts more deeply when they have opportunities to talk about varied representations and the math ideas they represent.

Exploring Math Representations

Through representations, students make their understanding visible. Representations in math class have many forms including:

- acting out math concepts/situations (such as showing 3 + 2 with 3 boys and 2 girls in front of the class, showing lines or angles with finger or hand movements, or indicating coordinate points by moving to points on a grid made with tape on the floor)
- concrete materials including commercial manipulatives or teacher- or student-made materials (such as 2-color counters, base-ten blocks, or strips of paper to represent various fractions)
- drawings or diagrams of math ideas (such as sticks and dots to represent tens and ones in place value activities or tree diagrams used to solve problems)
- virtual manipulatives that use advanced technology to make math ideas visible and moveable on the screen (such as interactive hundred charts or nets that can be "folded" into their corresponding three-dimensional figures)
- charts, tables, or graphs (including ratio tables and charts of data from class investigations)
- natural language as students describe math ideas with words (encouraging students to define concepts in their own words—we will explore this in Chapter 4)
- Numeric and symbolic representations including equations or inequalities.

Through representations, students make abstract ideas concrete and visible. In doing so, they are able to manipulate, communicate, analyze, and generalize about the math ideas.

CHOOSING, USING, AND INTERPRETING REPRESENTATIONS

Although a particular visual model may come to mind when we think about a math concept, our students do not necessarily picture math ideas in the same way we do and may not benefit as much from seeing our model as they would from creating their own. Our students build math understanding as they struggle to "picture" the math idea, whether they are acting it out, using concrete materials, or drawing diagrams. The goal is not to designate specific models that students must make but to allow students to create models, represent their ideas in varied ways, and then talk about, compare, and generalize to move beyond the models as they continue to explore the math ideas they represent.

Although commercially produced materials are a useful option, student-generated models are less expensive, serve the same purpose, and have the added advantage of being created by the students themselves. Although not as colorful or as exact as commercially produced materials, these models demonstrate our students' thinking. Drawing sticks and dots on paper to show tens and ones or cutting fractional parts from a paper square make easily accessible and appropriate tools for exploring and modeling math ideas. Students benefit from being introduced to certain materials (e.g., base-ten blocks to show place value) or certain ways to model problems (e.g., bar models or open number lines), but students should also have experiences in which they decide how to model their mathematical thinking.

In addition, students' experiences with models should include opportunities to interpret models—to determine what they might represent. Beginning lessons by having students interpret models provides engaging experiences that challenge them to think deeply about math ideas. Consider the following examples in which a model is shared and students talk with partners or teams to interpret it.

- A third-grade teacher placed 4 cubes on the table, 1 red and 3 blue. She wrote $\frac{1}{4}$ on the board and asked students to look at the cubes and decide what the 1 and 4 (numerator and denominator) represented.
- A fourth-grade teacher showed 0.1, 0.5, and 0.9 on 10 × 10 grids and asked students to figure out the connection between the numbers and models as in Figure 3.1.

Getting students involved in thinking, right from the start of the lesson, helps them make sense of the materials, the models, and the math.

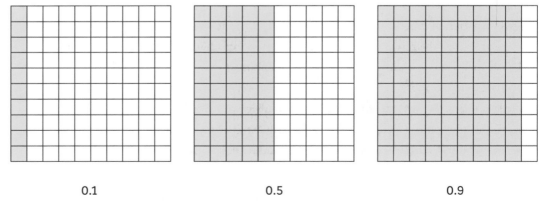

0.1   0.5   0.9

Figure 3.1 As students explore the diagrams and compare them to the numbers, they begin to make sense of the decimal notation.

When we engage students in creating and interpreting math representations, we are pushing them to think deeply about the math ideas. We are challenging them to visualize mathematics in different ways to explore, discuss, and make sense of it.

The Benefits of Representations

There are countless benefits to integrating representations into our math classrooms. Through representations our students:

- explore, visualize, and make sense of math concepts and processes
- strengthen their ability to communicate their mathematical thinking
- visualize, simplify, and solve math problems.

EXPLORING AND EXAMINING MATH CONCEPTS THROUGH REPRESENTATIONS

Representations allow our students to explore math concepts. They provide an entry point, as students visualize the skill or concept in a concrete way, and then provide opportunities for students to revisit and explore the skills and concepts to gain a deeper understanding. Through representations, our students are actively involved in exploring and making sense of math ideas.

Representations make abstract ideas visible. For many students, the abstract numbers and symbols of math don't mean anything. Through representations, they are able to see the math ideas and begin to make sense of them. As kindergarten students create chains of connecting cubes to represent the quantities 1–10 and then place them by a number strip, they see that each counting number represents 1 more than the number before it. This abstract concept becomes visible through their chains of cubes.

As third-grade students manipulate counters to show 3 rows of 5 cookies on a cookie sheet, then represent those cookies with circles in an array diagram, and finally connect the ideas to the expression 3 × 5, they are building understanding that begins with a model and moves to the abstract.

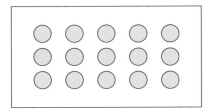

Representations make math learning active. When students are acting out equations, building models to compare numbers, testing for lines of symmetry (see Figure 3.2), or recording jumps on open number lines to show subtraction, they are actively involved in learning. As they make decisions about how to model ideas or investigate math concepts through concrete materials, they are doing mathematics. They are actively involved in constructing and demonstrating their understanding of math.

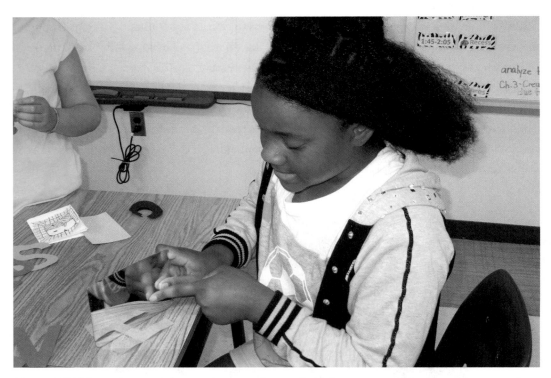

Figure 3.2 This student tests her conjectures about a line of symmetry using die-cut letters and mirrors.

Representations provide opportunities for students to delve into and deepen their understanding. As students work to create models of math ideas, their struggles are often evident. As they attempt to represent math concepts, they rethink ideas, listen to others, consider new perspectives, and build deeper understanding. Opportunities to step back, observe the models they create, and then discuss the math ideas those models represent allow them to discover important insights about how math works. As third graders cut out area models from grid paper to explore multiplication facts, they notice that the grid they cut out showing 3 rows of 5 can be rotated and now shows 5 rows of 3. Of course, there would be 15 squares in both models, the grid hasn't changed! The commutative property is visible. When kindergarten students see 7 represented in different ways on ten frames as in Figure 3.3, and then count to compare the number of counters on each frame, they discover that numbers can be arranged in different ways but still represent the same quantity.

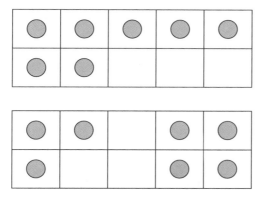

Figure 3.3 As students compare the two different representations of 7, they discover insights about how numbers work.

As fifth graders attempt to show their understanding of adding fractions with unlike denominators, they often start, stop, erase, and rethink until they find a way to show $\frac{1}{3} + \frac{1}{2}$ using pattern blocks (see Figure 3.4). This productive struggle results in a deeper understanding of equivalent fractions.

Figure 3.4 Students use pattern blocks to model fractions with unlike denominators as they struggle to understand how the fractions can be added.

Representations make math procedures observable. As students represent math processes like subtracting 2-digit numbers or adding decimals, they make sense of the computation process as they reflect and discuss their models. Fourth-grade students use many different models—number lines, diagrams, and concrete materials—to show adding fractions with like denominators. As they examine $\frac{1}{4} + \frac{2}{4} = \frac{3}{4}$ as in Figure 3.5, their models help them make sense of why the denominator does not change (their models show that the pieces are all fourths) and why the numerators are added together (by combining one-fourth and two-fourths, they now have three-fourths). Creating classrooms that nurture the use of representations provides students with many opportunities to analyze, discuss, and discover math ideas.

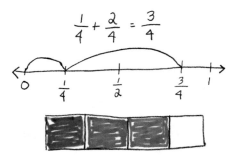

Figure 3.5 Students visualize adding fractions in different ways and are able to use the models to make sense of why they add the numerators and keep the denominators the same.

The Value of **Multiple Representations**

When creating models, choice is an important consideration, because we are asking students to make sense of their ideas and express their understandings. Selecting a model that works for them, but also deciphering how others chose to represent the same concept, strengthens their understanding of that concept. Having toolboxes available that offer students a choice of materials allows them to make decisions about how best to represent the math idea. A kindergarten teacher might offer students ten frames, counters, connecting cubes, and paper and pencil as options to show 7 and then ask students to explain to a partner how they know their model shows 7; a fourth-grade teacher might give students fraction bars, paper and pencil, pattern blocks, and Cuisenaire® rods to choose from as they work to model fraction addition. And, of course, justifying their choices, why they chose those materials or why they chose to represent the concept in the way they did, is an integral part of using models to enhance learning.

Creating models to show math ideas pushes our students to think about the math concepts, but the sharing of the models and the talk about what they show, how they could be modified, and how they are alike or different from other models truly deepens their understanding (see Figure 3.6). As students work with models, it is important that they talk about their decisions in creating the models, explain their models to others, ask questions about others' models, share what they notice as they compare models, and reveal their insights about commonalities and differences between varied models.

Figure 3.6 Students create varied models to show their understanding of geometric shapes. As students talk about and compare models, they gain insights and greater understanding.

As students examine multiple representations of the same concept, they uncover the big ideas that those representations share. For example:

- As students explore equivalent fractions, observing different models and looking for similarities and differences between them, they gain a deeper understanding of the concept of equivalence and gain insights (e.g., the numerator is half of the denominator), as in Figure 3.7.
- As students explore 0.50, whether using 10×10 grids or hundredths disks, they notice that 0.50 is always equivalent to 0.5 and has a value of $\frac{1}{2}$ (see Figure 3.8).

Figure 3.7 Students view equivalence in four different ways, deepening their understanding of the concept.

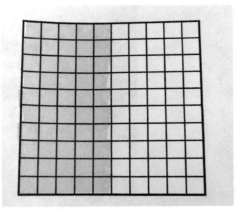 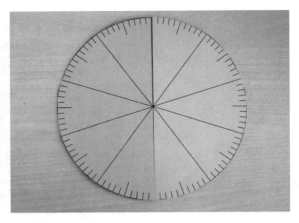

Figure 3.8 While the two models look different, they reveal the same insight about the value of the decimals, that 0.5 and 0.50 represent the same value.

Moving from Concrete to Abstract

By exploring math concepts through a variety of concrete and pictorial representations, our students build a foundation for ultimately understanding the abstract representations of math. Consider the development of students' understanding of place value, a critical understanding that allows them to figure out how numbers work.

To develop a deep understanding of place value, we offer a variety of tools for students to model and manipulate numbers, beginning with building a basic understanding of place value by having students bundle discrete (groupable) objects, like craft sticks or coffee stirrers, into tens and ones. As students grasp this idea, we introduce prebundled materials (like base-ten blocks), asking students to make sense of the materials by connecting these to the bundles they previously made. Although they no longer need to bundle their own groups of 10 or 100 items, they are still able to see that 10 individual units are the same as a rod, as they line 10 units next to a rod to confirm their thinking. In the same way, they line 10 rods next to a flat to confirm that 10 tens are the same as 1 hundred. As students explore with hands-on materials, we offer parallel activities that invite them to draw representations of the models and show the number values in standard form. By drawing sticks and dots or connecting the place value concepts to previously used models like number bonds, students are exploring place value concepts in a multitude of ways. And nonproportional models, such as number disks (circles of the same size labeled with values 1, 10, and 100), allow students to consider the place value ideas even when they cannot see the 10:1 ratio (see Figure 3.9). Each type of representation shows the same place value concepts, but the representations range from concrete to abstract (see Figure 3.10). Not all students need every type of representation to make sense of place value concepts, but some students benefit from a gentler transition from concrete to abstract so they can process and confirm their insights as they move toward abstract representation.

Inherent in this transition from one representation to the next is thoughtful discussion about each specific representation and about how one compares to another. When concrete materials are used one day and then pictorial or abstract representation is used the next, students often view them as two distinct ideas. Bridging from one type of representation to the next is a critical aspect of teaching through models. Recording pictorial models as students explore with counters or cubes, writing equations as they show math operations with diagrams, or having them frequently share and compare their varied representations helps them connect these different representations of the same math ideas. As students see their experiences written in symbolic form, or discussed in more abstract ways, they begin to see the connection between their concrete or pictorial experiences and the corresponding abstract ideas or symbols. Whether students are working with whole numbers, fractions, or decimals, exposure to varied models deepens their conceptual understanding.

Figure 3.9 After work with proportional base-ten blocks, this student demonstrates her understanding of place value using nonproportional number disks.

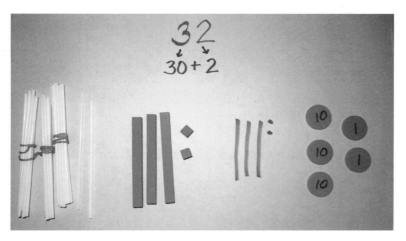

Figure 3.10 Students' experiences with concrete, pictorial, and number-based representations provide them with a strong understanding of place value concepts.

REPRESENTATIONS AS A COMMUNICATION TOOL

It is not easy for students to talk and write about their math ideas. The language of math is difficult and students often have a hard time finding just the right words to express their math thinking. Representations offer them another way to express those ideas. As they try to describe concepts like *parallel*, *congruent*, or *equivalent*, the ability to draw examples helps them communicate their thinking. As they attempt to justify why 1.5 is greater than 1.25, the ability to build a model helps them construct a convincing argument (see Figure 3.11). As students share their thinking with classmates, the ability to refer back to the concrete materials they used or share their diagram allows them to more easily explain their thinking and helps classmates better understand what they are sharing. Creating and sharing models helps our students find ways to get their thinking out of their heads.

When asked to describe symmetry, students might draw a diagram to show the concept. When asked to explain how they subtracted 3-digit numbers, they might refer to and explain their use of base-ten blocks. When asked to justify why $\frac{2}{3}$ is greater than $\frac{1}{4}$, they might use number line models to prove that their thinking makes sense.

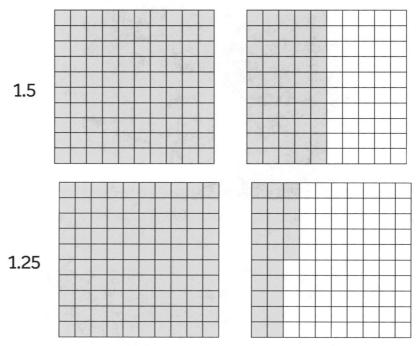

Figure 3.11 Shading and comparing 10 × 10 grids shows indisputably that 1.5 > 1.25.

For more on using representations to communicate about math, see Chapter 4.

REPRESENTATIONS AS A TOOL TO VISUALIZE AND SOLVE PROBLEMS

In Chapter 1, we talked about the importance of developing mathematical thinkers. We discussed ways to support our students to develop the thinking skills needed to be mathematical problem solvers. Before beginning to solve any math problem, our students' first task is to comprehend the problem. Visualizing is one strategy for doing this. Students might act out problems, use hands-on materials, draw pictures and diagrams, or show the problem using equations. In each case, they create representations of the problem situation to better understand it and to determine the math that is needed to find a solution.

Acting Out Problems

At all levels, acting out problems brings them to life. Primary students act out simple addition problems as 4 students are seated at a table and 1 more student joins them. They are able to visualize the concept of adding 1. Intermediate students might act out multiplication or division problems, forming arrays of students to demonstrate 2×5 or $10 \div 2$. Through actively modeling the problems, students are able to feel the actions of the operations as they move in and out of groups or as they arrange themselves in various formations to match the problem situations.

Using Concrete Materials and Drawings to Visualize Problems

Real objects allow students to explore problems by manipulating the data. Primary students explore that 3 pencils plus 2 pencils is 5 pencils by placing the pencils on their table and putting the two groups together. Then, they begin to use cubes or counters to represent the real items, not needing the actual pencils but still benefiting from the concrete objects and the ability to move them together. Organizers like part-part-whole mats allow students to continue to explore the idea of addition as they place counters in the *parts* sections and make observations about what it means to add as they move them together to the *whole* section (see Figure 3.12).

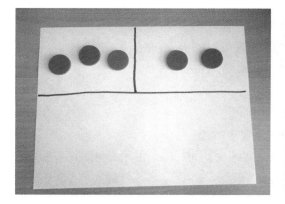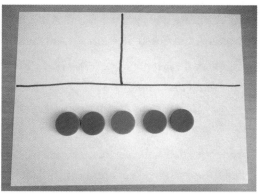

Figure 3.12 The part-part-whole mat allows students to visualize addition as *putting together* as they see the two parts being combined to create the whole.

Visualizing with Diagrams: Number Bonds, Place Value Models, and Bar Models

Drawings are also key tools for visualizing problems and, as with physical objects, our students move from more concrete and situation-specific representations to more abstract ones. For instance, as kindergarten students try to determine how many animals are at a farm that has 4 cows and 2 horses, their first pictures are generally realistic as they attempt to draw each cow and horse. Soon, with our encouragement, our students transition to showing the cows and horses with circles or other abstract representations (see Figure 3.13), understanding that the diagrams we use to solve problems don't require the detail of an art project.

Figure 3.13 Students draw 4 cows and 2 horses and count to find the total, then transition to drawing circles to represent cows and horses as they begin to connect the symbolic representation (equation) to the story.

Students can then move to even more abstract representations, like number bonds, which allow them to show ideas without moving counters on a part-part-whole mat, or drawing circles to represent each object (see Figure 3.14). Introducing these new models through think-aloud techniques and questions pulls students into the process of making sense of them.

What if I just put the number here rather than using the counters?
Would that work? Why?
How is it like our part-part-whole mat? How is it different?
When might this be a helpful way to show a problem? Why?

Through partner and class discussions, we continue to stretch our students' thinking to consider different ways to represent problem situations.

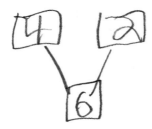

Figure 3.14 Students might choose to represent the parts and whole with number bonds rather than placing counters on a part-part-whole mat.

Another way to support students in drawing reasonable models is through the use of place value models to represent the data, as in Figure 3.15. As problem data increase, students who are still drawing every individual item are likely to make errors in representing or counting the individual items they have drawn. And our goal is to move students from counting to adding using place value strategies. Representing the data with place value representations (sticks and dots) allows the students to find the tens and ones and combine them to find the sum. To help students transition from drawing discrete objects, we might begin class discussions about whether it is getting hard to draw all of the items and ask students for suggestions as to how to simplify their drawings. We might select a piece of student work that shows a more efficient model and share that work with others, asking the student to explain her model.

Bar models are another option for modeling problems without drawing discrete objects (see Figure 3.16). Like other diagrams, they can be used in different ways depending on the problem

Figure 3.15 Rather than drawing 36 separate stickers, this student chooses to represent the problem data with sticks and dots, allowing him to use his place value understanding to find the sum.

and the way a student thinks about it. Consider the different ways the following problem is diagrammed.

Mr. Johnson's class was going on a hike. He packed 24 oatmeal granola bars and 28 peanut granola bars in his backpack. How many granola bars were in his backpack?

Figure 3.16 Both bar models show the addition situation and help the students visualize the total number of granola bars.

Bar models are equally useful for representing multiplication and division situations. Initially, students gain conceptual understanding of multiplication by using concrete objects (counters or square tiles) to build set models, arrays, or area models and then find the total objects or gain conceptual understanding of division by separating a total into equal groups or rows. Students transition to modeling problem situations by drawing the sets, arrays, or area models. Bar models continue to be helpful as students explore these operations (see Figure 3.17). And bar models are an effective way to introduce and explore multiplicative comparison problems as in Figure 3.18.

There are 4 wreaths with 10 pine cones on each wreath. How many pine cones are there?

If 24 cookies are shared equally among 3 children, how many cookies will each child get?

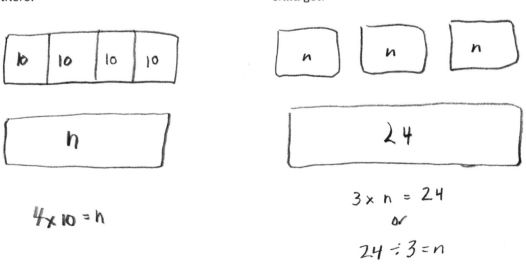

Figure 3.17 As students construct bar models, they are analyzing the problem situation to identify the operation and build an appropriate equation.

The bush was 4 feet tall. The tree was 5 times as tall as the bush. How tall was the tree?

The tree was 20 feet tall. The tree was 5 times as tall as the bush. How tall was the bush?

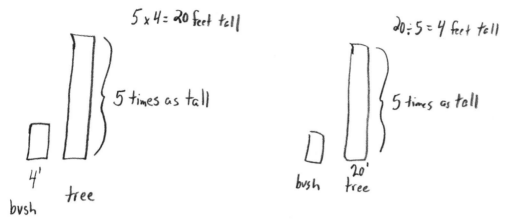

Figure 3.18 Multiplicative comparison problems become easier to understand when they can be visualized.

REPRESENTATIONS TO EXPLORE UNKNOWNS IN DIFFERENT POSITIONS

Representations like part-part-whole mats, number bonds, and bar models are a tremendous support to students who struggle with the concept of unknowns in different positions in a problem. Beginning by diagramming the problem and placing a question mark (?) where the unknown appears, they can use their understanding of the model to build an equation with an unknown. This often allows them to move through their initial confusion when start data or change data are unknown (see Figures 3.19 and 3.20).

There were 5 lemon lollipops and some grape lollipops. There were 8 lollipops altogether. How many were grape?

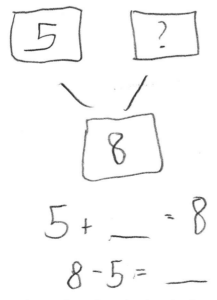

Figure 3.19 Students' understanding of number bonds allows them to show problem data with an unknown in any position and then transition to an equation that shows the relationship between the three numbers.

Ellen had some strawberries.
Mom gave her 4 more. Then she had 11.
How many strawberries did she have to start?

Ellen had 7 strawberries.
Mom gave her some more. Then she had 11.
How many strawberries did Mom give her?

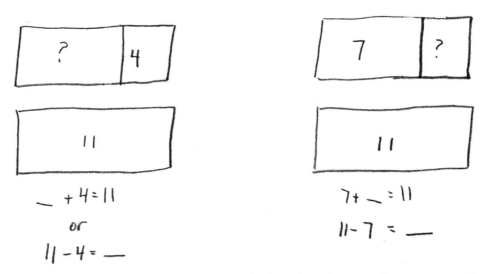

Figure 3.20 With bar models, students can simply show the unknown with a question mark and then build the equation(s) to represent the situation.

As students create their models to show the math problem, they build equations to represent it as well, strengthening their understanding of the connections between the visual models and the abstract symbolic representation. Having the models and equations side by side allows them to compare the parts of the equation to their visual representations to gain greater expertise and confidence with abstract representations. Frequently asking students to explain how the numbers in the equation are connected to the model and to the problem helps them connect the visual, abstract, and contextual representations.

> *What does the 4 represent?*
> *What does the 11 represent?*
> *What is unknown? Where is it in your diagram?*
> *How did your diagram help you figure out which operation made sense?*

For more ideas on connecting equations and problem situations, see Chapter 2.

Number Lines

Number lines are another helpful way to represent math problems. Initially number lines may be simple as in the 1–15 number line in Figure 3.21. The student is able to use the number line to visualize and solve an addition problem with an unknown addend.

As data gain complexity, students might create open number lines, starting and ending at any points that make sense for the problem. Students can move forward or backward on number lines, showing addition or subtraction. And unlike bar diagrams, number lines provide computational support by allowing students to decompose numbers to find ways of simplifying the addition or subtraction process (see Figure 3.22).

Spring Flowers

Annie had 8 flowers.
Molly gave her some more flowers.
Now Annie has 12 flowers.
How many did Molly give her?

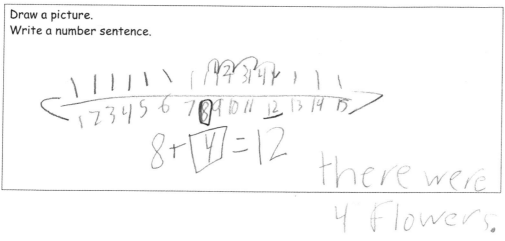

Figure 3.21 This student effectively uses a number line to count on to find the missing addend.

Lots of Stickers

Molly had **47** stickers. She had **12 more** stickers than Colin. How many stickers did Colin have? Write an equation and show how you got the answer.

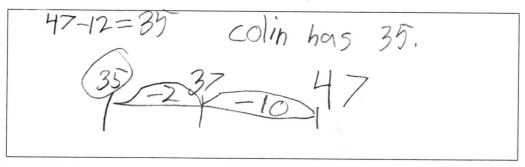

Figure 3.22 This student begins at 47, then subtracts 10 and 2 more to find that Colin had 35 stickers. She might have decomposed 12 in other ways (e.g., subtracting 7 to land on 40, then subtracting 5 more).

Showing equal jumps on number lines is an effective way to model multiplication and division (see Figures 3.23 and 3.24).

Jason ran 6 miles. He ran 2 miles each day. How many days did he run?

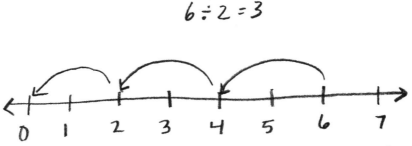

$$6 \div 2 = 3$$

Figure 3.23 Division is represented through equal jumps on the number line, revealing 3 jumps of 2 miles each.

5 runners ran a relay race. Each one ran $\frac{1}{4}$ mile. How long was the race?

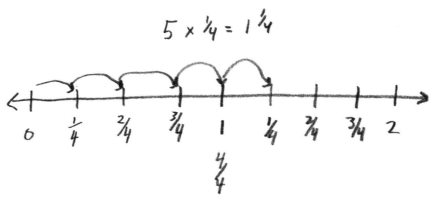

$$5 \times \tfrac{1}{4} = 1\tfrac{1}{4}$$

Figure 3.24 Multiplications of a whole number by a fraction is represented on the number line, helping students realize the connection to models for multiplication with whole numbers.

Diagrams as a Problem-Solving Strategy

As students explore the various problem structures for addition, subtraction, multiplication, and division (see Chapter 2), their representations help them visualize each structure, seeing the actions or comparisons that are the hallmark for each operation. As they explore each operation, beginning with problem situations, representing them from concrete to pictorial to abstract, and discussing and forming generalizations about the situations that show each operation, they are developing an in-depth understanding of the operations.

But this is not the only way students can use visualization as a problem-solving strategy. Using representations like tables, charts, and organized lists can be quite an effective problem-solving strategy for other kinds of problems.

Visualizing to Simplify

Some problems appear particularly confusing when first read, but visualizing these problems helps to simplify them. Consider the problem in Figure 3.25.

The Lemonade Problem

Kelly was in line to buy lemonade.

There were 3 people in front of her in the line.

There were 2 people behind her in the line.

How many people were waiting in line to buy lemonade?

Figure 3.25 Drawing a diagram allows students to catch their mental errors.

A very common but incorrect answer to this problem is 5 because students see the 3 and 2 in the problem and add them. But when they model the problem, they can see that Kelly was in the line too and add 3 + 1 + 2 or just draw and count the 6 people in line.

For other problems, a simple tree diagram can make a confusing situation clearer (see Figure 3.26).

The fifth grade had a phone tree to get important messages to all of the students. Their teacher, Mrs. Wilson, phoned 3 students. Those students each phoned 3 students, and then those students each phoned 2 students. How many students received a phone call?

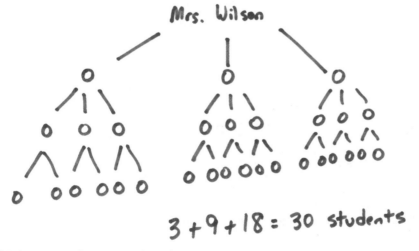

Figure 3.26 Creating a diagram to show the problem situation clarifies the situation and makes the solution evident.

Although this problem appears quite confusing after the first read, with the help of a tree diagram, the confusion dissolves and students need only be able to count to get the correct answer.

VISUALIZING TO FIND PATTERNS

Creating data representations on charts and tables allows students to see patterns and functions within the data. For example, students were stymied when trying to figure out how many sections would appear if a sheet of paper were folded in half 8 times when they couldn't make more than 5 actual folds. They recorded their data on a table, examined the organized data for patterns, and discovered that with every fold the sections doubled. Their insight allowed them to find the solution (see Figure 3.27).

If you folded a square piece of paper in half 8 times, how many sections would be on the paper?

folds	1	2	3	4	5	6	7	8
sections	2	4	8	16	32	64	128	256

Figure 3.27 By representing their data on an organized table, students are able to discover a pattern that leads them to the solution.

Through representations of math ideas, our students are better able to visualize and examine math concepts and solve math problems—and communicate their thinking and solutions. In the next chapter, we explore this important aspect of math teaching as we examine the role of talk and writing in math class.

Tips for Representations

Number of the Day

Provide frequent opportunities for students to show their understanding of numbers through varied representations with a Number of the Day (see Figure 3.28). Pose a number appropriate for the grade level (e.g., 10 for kindergartners, 126 for second graders, $\frac{1}{4}$ for third graders, 0.4 for fourth graders) and have students show the number in as many ways as possible. Encourage students to use pictures, diagrams, words, and abstract representations. Post their work for classmates to see or have them share their ideas with partners or teams.

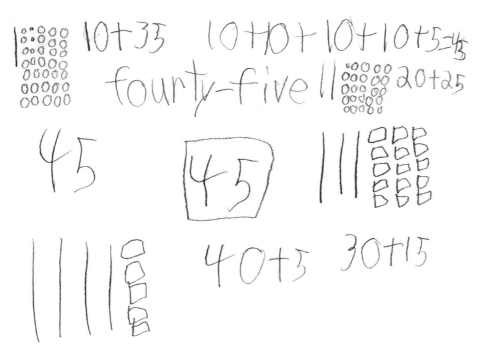

Figure 3.28 This student shows his understanding of 45 in multiple ways.

Create Toolboxes

Consider having math toolboxes for students to use during classroom lessons. Depending on the grade level, toolboxes might include counters, cubes, dry erase boards, number lines, hundred charts, calculators, or materials specific to a topic (e.g., place value mats, fraction pieces, decimal grids). Having a box of supplies allows students to make choices as they represent and explore math ideas and ensures that materials are available when needed.

Encourage Labeling

Understanding what a model represents is a critical part of using it effectively. If drawing bar models to show comparisons, it is important to know what each bar represents. If creating comparison models with connecting cubes, labeling the towers with sticky notes helps to clarify what each tower represents. Get students used to labeling their representations to be sure they interpret them correctly and to allow others to understand what they represent.

Use Color, Arrows, and Circles to Highlight Ideas and Processes

Use different colors when modeling ideas on the board. The use of color makes ideas more visible to students, as in Figure 3.29. Draw students' attention to specific numbers with arrows or circles, as in Figure 3.30. Encourage students to incorporate color or arrows in their diagrams to make their actions visible.

continues

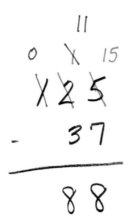

Figure 3.29 The use of color allows students to distinguish the steps in the subtraction process.

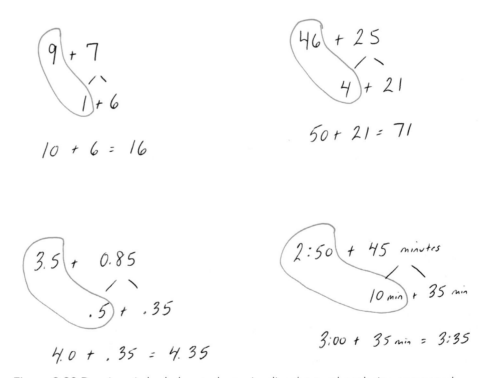

Figure 3.30 Drawing circles helps students visualize the numbers being composed.

Building Strong Bridges

Record numbers and equations next to concrete or pictorial models. As students see the symbolic form, they begin to grasp the connection between their concrete or pictorial experiences and the abstract representations.

Explore Virtual Manipulatives

There are many outstanding virtual manipulatives available online. Interactive whiteboards allow us to drag base-ten materials as we compose tens or highlight hundred charts to show patterns. Three-dimensional objects can be rotated and unfolded to show their nets. These virtual manipulatives add a great deal to our math lessons, but they are not a replacement for hands-on experiences. Students need to have materials in their hands and explore the making of mathematical models.

Reflect and Record

After creating models, students should be given opportunities to talk about their models, share them with others, compare various models, and summarize their learning. Primary students might draw and label what was done, and intermediate students could write about their observations and insights. Reflecting on their learning brings closure to the experience.

 Scan this QR code or visit http://hein.pub/MathinPractice to see videos related to students using representations and to access additional online resources (use keycode MIPGT).

Study Group Questions

1. Why should students be given opportunities to create their own models? How can you make that happen with your students?
2. What is the benefit of students' exploring varied models?
3. How can you bridge students' experiences between concrete, representational, and abstract models? Why is it important to do that?
4. What is the role of models in solving math problems? How can you help your students model problems more effectively?
5. How can models support students as they talk and write about their math ideas?

Talk About It, Write It Down

Getting Students Communicating About Math

We have long recognized the important role talk and writing play in students' learning. As students talk and write, they

- process ideas
- identify misconceptions
- rethink ideas and reconsider strategies
- make connections between ideas and methods
- develop insights.

In all content areas, communication (verbal, visual, and written) is central to learning, although math teachers have not historically taken advantage of the benefits of mathematical discourse. Today's teachers, however, recognize that math learning happens when students are talking. As our students explain and describe their math ideas, they are processing, organizing, reconsidering, analyzing, justifying, summarizing, and testing conjectures. They are making sense of math.

The importance of mathematical discourse is evident in every chapter of this book. We have discussed the importance of asking our students thoughtful questions, the benefits of students discovering math concepts through investigations and discussions, and the importance of students describing and comparing the models they use to visualize and explore math ideas. Our students benefit from being challenged to talk, draw, and write about the math they are learning. Through this discourse, they learn to think like mathematicians.

Our goal is both to help our students learn math through discourse and to help them become more skilled at that discourse. It is often difficult for our students to find the words to express math thinking or to know how to adequately answer deep questions. And without precision, our students' comments do not have the substance to develop deep thinking. In this chapter, we will discuss ways to generate productive math talk and ways to help students develop the language of math as they learn to talk and write about math.

What the Research, Standards, and Experts Say About Communicating in Math Class

NCTM has identified communication as one of its five process standards through which students explore and use mathematics. And in *Principles to Actions* (2014), NCTM recommends "facilitate meaningful mathematical discourse" as one of its eight key mathematics teaching practices. The Common Core (2010) also recognizes the importance of communication in the third Standard for Mathematical Practice: "Construct viable arguments and critique the arguments of others." And as we look more deeply at the Standards for Mathematical Practice, we realize that none of them could be developed without math talk. How can you help students make sense of math problems, construct arguments, model in varied ways, select appropriate tools, recognize patterns and properties, or develop rules or generalizations without math talk? All these documents recognize that through discourse, students organize and refine their thinking, analyze and evaluate the thinking of others, and communicate their understanding to peers. Discourse promotes deep learning of mathematics.

Engaging students in productive talk about their math experiences has been shown to enhance student learning (Stein and Smith 2011). Talk in math class advances student learning both directly, through opportunities for students to discuss math strategies, methods, and concepts, and indirectly, through the development of a learning community in which students learn from one another through respectful and productive discourse (Chapin, O'Connor, and Anderson 2009). When students are given rich math tasks and we have high expectations for meaningful talk about the tasks, they are able to generate deep mathematical thinking (Spangler et al. 2014). We have discussed the importance of students creating models, but the opportunity to talk about what they are doing and why they are doing it is an essential part of that process (National Research Council 2009). Over and over we hear the evidence that mathematical discourse promotes student learning. Rather than using talk and writing just to check comprehension, our goal is to use it to develop, test, and share mathematical thinking.

Generating Math Talk

Our role in promoting mathematical discourse is flexible. At times, we pose the questions, select specific students to share their thinking, and rephrase, clarify, and sequence the learning as we stay in control of managing the discourse. At other times, we relinquish that control to offer students opportunities to carry the math conversations, ask the questions, and challenge others' thinking. By finding a balance between orchestrating discussions and guiding student-led conversations, we provide students with balanced opportunities to communicate their mathematical thinking.

So, how do we get the full advantage of talk in our classrooms? What can we do to maximize the benefits for our students? Consider the following:

1. Create a classroom climate conducive to math talk.
2. Provide varied and ongoing opportunities for math talk.
3. Teach students what productive talk sounds like, and how to listen to each other.

CREATING THE CLIMATE

Math conversations thrive when students feel safe to share their ideas. When students are anxious that they will be judged, they hesitate to contribute to discussions. And often, those students most need to talk about their ideas so they can process them and make sense of the math concepts.

We work to create an environment in which our students feel free to comment and question and in which learning through discourse can take place. And our expectations and actions should match our goals.

- If we want students to talk, we should expect some noise within the classroom.
- If we want on-task behavior, we move through the room and monitor student talk to be sure it is on topic and productive.
- If we expect math talk to reveal insights and misconceptions, we listen as students talk.
- If we want to encourage reluctant students to join class conversations, we allow wait time, allow them to process their ideas with partners before class sharing, and sequence the sharing to allow reluctant students to share insights early in the discussions so their answers are acknowledged and their participation is rewarded.
- If we want to show the value of different perspectives and methods, we highlight several approaches and make connections among the varied ideas shared.
- If we expect students to comment and critique each other's thinking, we ask them to respond to others' thinking and discuss respectful ways for them to disagree.

We work to find ways to create an environment in which sharing ideas is valued, regardless of whether those ideas are right or wrong. We help our students appreciate that talking about math leads to discovery and understanding (see Figure 4.1).

Figure 4.1 When students talk about math, they discover ideas and are actively involved in learning.

Tips for Creating a Climate Conducive to Math Talk

Physical Setup

Arrange classroom seating so math talk can happen throughout the lesson. When chairs must be moved or students must be reseated, the frequency of classroom talk diminishes. Arranging desks in pairs or groups so quick discussions can occur at any time maximizes the use of math talk throughout the lesson.

Partner Talk

Rather than posing a problem for one student to answer, consider asking students to turn and share their responses with partners. As they talk with partners, students articulate and process their ideas in a less threatening way and are then better prepared for participation in whole-class discussions.

continues

Allow Wait Time

Allow wait time for students to formulate their ideas before asking them to share with the class. Simple techniques like think-pair-share in which students (1) think silently about the question, (2) share their ideas with partners, and then (3) share their thinking with the whole class ensure that all students have time to process their own ideas before being asked to share them with the class.

Promote Active Listening

Ask students to retell or elaborate on other students' responses. To restate what others say or add on to their ideas, students must listen closely to each other and they become active listeners. And when they really listen to each other, insights occur.

Emphasize Process

Deemphasize the importance of the answer and emphasize the importance of the thinking or process. The answer is valued in math, but so is the thinking that leads us to that answer. Asking students to explain their thinking and praising their methods helps them realize that the answer is not all we are evaluating.

Acknowledge the Value of Errors

Acknowledge that wrong answers lead to right answers and that thinking often needs to be modified. Students need to hear that everyone makes mistakes and that they are a part of the learning process. By allowing students to change their mind or adapt their answer during the course of a lesson, we are helping them see that wrong answers happen and that they are a part of the learning process.

PROVIDING OPPORTUNITIES FOR MATH TALK

Math talk takes many forms in K–5 classrooms. We can use math discourse to develop and extend students' thinking during whole-class discussions, small teacher-led groups, partner sharing, collaborative teams, and class presentations.

Whole-Class Discussions

Although these discussions were once characterized by teacher-to-student discourse, today we work to build the expectation that students are listening to each other's comments and that student-to-student conversations are a part of the mix. To support these goals, we

- conduct frequent partner sharing in the midst of whole-class discussions or debates
- defer students' questions to other classmates to answer
- ask students to comment on each other's ideas.

Whole-class discussions are no longer characterized by the teacher asking a question with one student answering it; instead, they are filled with discussions between and among the students and teacher.

Small Teacher-Led Groups

Small teacher-led groups are intimate learning sessions. The smaller student-to-teacher ratio means that each student is actively involved and able to frequently share his ideas. It often feels less threatening for students to share their ideas in front of these small groups rather than in front of the whole class. And because these small groups are often like-ability groups, students are being asked to talk about ideas that are at their level and are then able to have meaningful conversations with others at the same level. In small teacher-led groups, students are consistently talking about their thinking, and the teacher is able to probe with specific questions to clarify and extend their understanding and challenge them to make sense of the math ideas.

For more on differentiating instruction through varied grouping formats, see Chapter 5.

Collaborative Groups

Our students benefit from opportunities to talk to each other, discuss and debate math ideas, and ask and answer each other's questions (NCTM 2014). And students benefit from opportunities to do this without the teacher leading the discussion. Through partner and team tasks, our students have opportunities to take responsibility for the discourse. But how can we ensure that these student-to-student conversations are productive? What can we do to maximize these opportunities?

One of the most frustrating parts of student-to-student discourse is our students' tendency to stray from the math topic. Setting expectations about math talk is essential. Stress that it is everyone's responsibility to keep discussions on target. All students are expected to share ideas. Partners are expected to talk respectfully to each other. Disagreement is expected to happen, but arguments should not.

Involve students in developing expectations for math talk. Have them work in teams to discuss the behaviors that lead to productive and respectful discussions. Guiding questions like the following can help to focus these discussions:

- What should you be talking about?
- Who should share ideas?
- What should you be doing while others are talking?
- What if you disagree? How should you share your different idea?

After teams have had a chance to discuss their ideas, have them share their thoughts with the class. Ask them for examples, or to clarify their comments, so the important ideas surface (e.g., Why do we want everyone to share ideas? What if someone keeps interrupting? How could you disagree nicely? What would that sound like?). Summarize and record their thoughts on a class chart to remind them of the expectations for productive, respectful, and equitable group discussions (see Figure 4.2). Refer to the chart before collaborative team tasks to focus students on expected behaviors, and have teams revisit the chart after team tasks to evaluate their talk.

Collaborative groups require our active participation to ensure productive talk. Here are some ways we can support student groups before, during, and after a collaborative task.

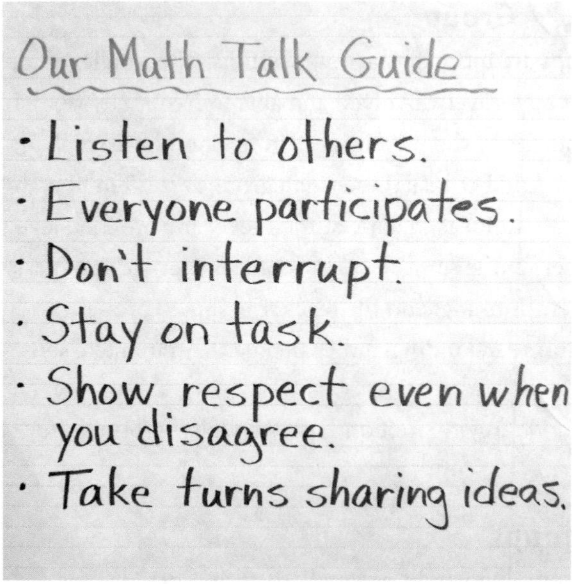

Figure 4.2 The expectations for math talk are generated by students and used to guide their group discussions.

Before

- Provide clear directions for the task and ask students to restate them before getting started.
- Establish clear expectation for equitable participation in the group, including giving roles to each student (e.g., leader, recorder, reporter) or having a system in which students place a counter or cube in the center as they share an idea and when all counters are in the center, they can collect them and start again.

During

- Move through the room to ensure that students are on task and monitor their progress toward completing the task.
- Listen to team discussions and notice strategies, making note of those that should be a part of the class debriefing. Which strategies would make for a good start to the class sharing? How do other strategies connect to the more basic strategies? What would be a good progression for sharing and making connections between the strategies?

After

- Debrief about the math, having teams share answers and methods. Teams might report to the class or display models or posters followed by a gallery walk to view each group's work. Team sharing should include discussion of times when they may have gotten stuck and how they got unstuck to finally complete the task or solve the problem.
- Praise math ideas and insights, but also praise productive math talk, sharing comments that were overheard, from respectfully questioning each other's ideas to asking their teammates for clarification about their ideas.

- Have teams discuss their math talk with feedback forms or prompts like:
  - Did we stay on task?
  - Did everyone share ideas?
  - Did we listen to each other?
  - Were we respectful of each other's ideas?

Perhaps one of the most difficult things we do as teachers is to let go of the control during these student-to-student discussions (see Figure 4.3). Letting them struggle rather than providing a quick rescue can be difficult, but it is often through productive struggle and making mistakes that our students finally reach solutions. Taking a step back from showing or telling students how to do math to allow them to discuss, debate, and find ways that make sense to them can be unnerving, but learning to think mathematically entails ups and downs, misinformed strategies, and erroneous conclusions. Through our whole-class debriefings, we are able to clarify misconceptions, discuss the efficiency of strategies, and identify important skills and concepts.

Figure 4.3 Students thrive on opportunities to talk about math with classmates.

Presentations/Sharing

Orchestrating opportunities for our students to share their methods for solving a problem or their insights after a class investigation provides them with an important chance to express their math thinking.

- Can they find the best words to share their ideas?
- Can they design a model or diagram to help others better understand their strategies?
- Can they build convincing arguments to make their points?

Students might use materials to show how they found an answer (see Figure 4.4) or record their method on whiteboards to share with the class (see Figure 4.5). Sharing their ideas forces students to reflect on what they did and why they did it and then to find an effective way to communicate that to others. It pushes students to delve into their own thinking.

Figure 4.4 This student explains how she used pattern blocks to solve a problem requiring adding fractions with unlike denominators.

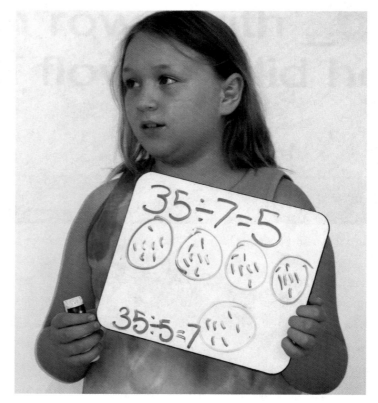

Figure 4.5 This student shares her model, her solution, and her method with the class.

TEACHING PRODUCTIVE TALK

For students to be comfortable and productive during math conversations, they must learn ways to begin conversations, ask questions, critique others' comments, and summarize their learning. To help them feel more comfortable interjecting comments in math discussions, many teachers highlight productive talk, suggesting and posting discussion starters to help students develop the habits of productive math talk.

Consider the following possibilities:

I agree with _____ because . . .

I disagree with _____ because . . .

That reminds me of . . .

I think _____ said . . .

I would like to add . . .

I don't understand . . .

Could you explain . . . ?

I have a question about . . .

During math discussions, remind students to refer to the list if they are struggling with how to interject comments into the conversations.

It is helpful to have discussions about what it sounds like to talk with respect. Some teachers facilitate class discussions and make lists of disrespectful ways (You are wrong!) and respectful ways (I think that . . .) to comment on each other's ideas. Because the tone of the comment can sometimes be more offensive than the words, role-play can be a good way to open discussions about our tone when we make comments. "That is not right" can sound quite differently depending on the tone in which it is said.

Students who are taught how to engage in productive math conversations, and who are praised for the quality and tone of their comments, develop valuable communication skills. And when students have effective communication skills, math talk is an invaluable learning tool.

Developing the Language of Math

We recognize the value of mathematical discourse, but what happens when our students can't find the words to express their math thinking? How can they explain, describe, justify, and summarize math ideas when they struggle to put their thinking into words? And are they truly understanding our teaching if they are unsure of the words we use as we explain and describe math ideas? To understand what we teach, and to express their own thinking, our students need to understand the language of math.

Specialized math vocabulary, including symbols and abbreviations, is not a part of our students' everyday experiences and must be developed within the classroom so that students can understand and use the appropriate words and symbols as they process information and communicate about math concepts. Research studies indicate the benefits of vocabulary instruction, including its positive impact on the comprehension of new content, and suggest that vocabulary instruction should include repeated exposure to words, instruction in new words, visual images to enhance retention of words, and a focus on those words that are critical to content (Marzano, Pickering, and Pollock 2001). Because students often struggle to find just the right word to express their mathematical thinking, supporting them to develop the language of math enhances their ability to precisely convey meaning (encouraged by the Common Core Standard for Mathematical Practice 6: Attend to precision). We support our students in developing the language of math by:

- introducing new words and symbols
- providing opportunities for them to explore words in context
- setting an expectation of precision when communicating about math.

INTRODUCING MATH WORDS AND SYMBOLS

Learning new vocabulary is not about copying a definition from a dictionary or glossary, because many students have no idea what dictionary definitions are saying. It is about introducing words through visuals, synonyms, examples, and connections to words students already know. It is about highlighting new words through charts, discussions, and interactive activities. And it is always about developing words in context, so the words and their meanings are learned together.

When students enter school, they experience a new language as they begin to learn mathematics; new words are introduced as each new concept is explored. Some are familiar words that now have new meanings related to mathematics (i.e., *feet* or *operation*). Others, like *place value* or *divisor*, are unique to the study of mathematics. It is easy to forget that the words we are using in our lessons may have little to no meaning to our students. As we plan math lessons, we consider ways to introduce or revisit important math words and symbols that will impact our students' understanding of and ability to communicate about the math they are learning.

In each module of the grade-level books, a list of vocabulary words related to the content is highlighted. Consider these words and whether they may be new to your students. Would your students benefit from a focus on these words and their meanings?

Prior to lessons, consider which words or symbols may be new to your students. Plan to introduce or revisit those words as a part of the lesson, being sure that the introduction is understandable to students.

- Can you show a *picture or diagram* that helps explain the meaning, such as a diagram to show symmetry or base-ten blocks to show tenths and hundredths?
- Are there *synonyms* that may build understanding (e.g., when we *decompose* a number, we break it apart)?
- Are you using *familiar words* in your introduction? Rather than simply defining a rhombus as a quadrilateral with congruent sides, you might need to restate *congruent* as "the length of the sides is equal" for those who might be lost in the technical language.

- Would *examples* make the meaning evident (e.g., comparing a sphere to a basketball or globe)?
- Are there *connections* to similar concepts (e.g., hundredths are parts of a whole, like tenths, but they're even smaller)?

As we introduce new math concepts, we pause to talk about significant words related to that content, record them so students can see them in written form, and illustrate or describe them. In this way, the words are introduced in context as we explore the related math content.

Utilizing Math Talk Charts and Word Walls

Math Talk charts and word walls are ways to highlight words for ongoing student reference. Both are displays of math vocabulary words that are constructed collaboratively with students. As new words or symbols appear in lessons, the teacher stops to record and discuss the word and its meaning. For word walls, the words might simply be recorded on a sentence strip and then placed on the wall. A visual might be added to the word card to briefly illustrate its meaning (see Figure 4.6). As we place the word card on the wall, we ask students to discuss its meaning or share examples or synonyms for the word. We make connections between the new word and other words on the wall and place the words in proximity to those that have connected meanings.

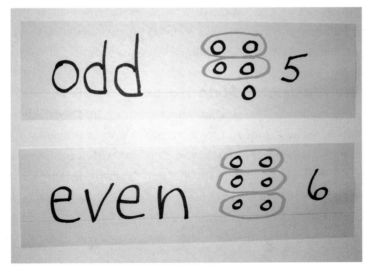

Figure 4.6 Word walls are created with students as we record the word, talk about its meaning, and place it on the wall for future reference.

Math Talk charts take word walls a step farther in that they provide more room to record phrases, draw diagrams, and display connected words (see Figure 4.7). A picture of a *pentagon*, a *right angle*, or *parallel lines* placed next to the words help students remember and retain meanings. Beginning a Math Talk chart for a specific concept, and then adding to it as related words are introduced, provides an organized reference chart containing not just words, but math concepts and connections.

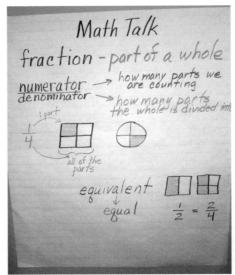
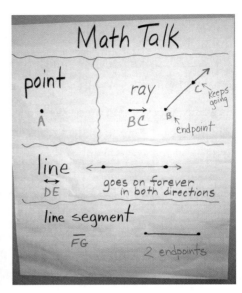

Figure 4.7 Math Talk charts provide a place to record related vocabulary along with phrases, diagrams, and examples that clarify the meanings.

Having words on classroom walls provides reference support for students who are unable to remember a word on their own. They foster precision as students are able to pinpoint the important words related to the math concepts they are learning and discussing, and they support students' independence as they find just the right words to effectively talk and write about their math ideas. Math Talk charts and word walls are strong instructional tools that allow students at all grade levels to visualize words, see connections between words, and explore word meanings.

Explaining and Illustrating Math Words

Along with recording key words on class charts and facilitating class discussions about the meanings of the words, we help students process the new words by providing opportunities to talk and write about them. Rather than just having students watch the teacher write the word, having them talk with partners about the new word and then write it along with their understanding of its meaning through words, pictures, and examples, helps students process the ideas, internalize the words, and better retain the words and their meanings. Folded books, organizers, and vocabulary logs are options for having students record their new understanding.

Folded Books

Challenge students to show their understanding of math words or symbols by making folded math books. Fold paper in varied ways to create small books to explore and illustrate math terms or concepts (shown in Figures 4.8 and 4.9).

- A two-fold book might ask students to define odd/even, add/subtract, fraction/decimal, or prime/composite.
- A three-fold book might ask students to write about inch/feet/yard, one/two/three, >/</=, standard form/word form/expanded form, or tenth/hundredth/thousandth.
- A four-fold book might ask students to write about circle/triangle/rectangle/square, penny/ nickel/dime/quarter, or ones/tens/hundreds/thousands.

Students record their ideas inside the flaps using words, pictures, numbers, and/or examples.

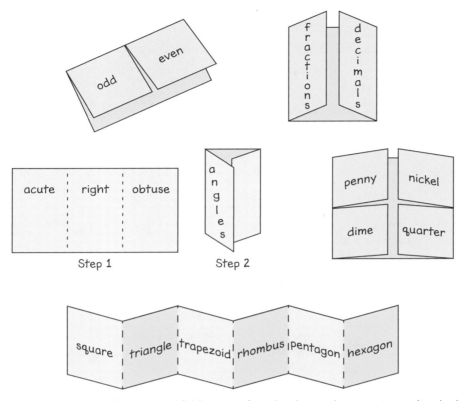

Figure 4.8 By using colored paper and folding it to form books, students are immediately drawn to the activity of describing and illustrating math ideas.

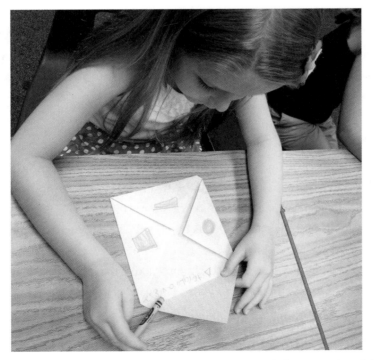

Figure 4.9 Students share their understanding of two-dimensional shapes in their folded books using pictures, words, numbers, and examples to describe the shapes.

ORGANIZERS

A word box is a simple math organizer that gets students thinking about new words in multiple ways. Students are given a math word and a word box and complete each section of the box to show their understanding of the highlighted word. The sections of the box might ask students to define, illustrate, provide an example, and list related words. Word boxes can be displayed on bulletin boards or compiled into individual, or class, books.

Variation: Rather than using the word box template, simply have students fold a piece of paper into four sections and tell them (or indicate with a template on the board) what should be recorded in each section. If time is limited, or to differentiate, have students fold their papers in two or three sections and select just two or three ways (e.g., define, illustrate, list related words) for the students to show their understanding of the word.

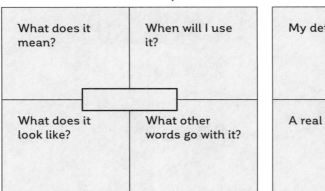
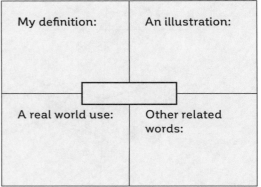

VOCABULARY LOGS

After discussing a new word in class, students record the word and its meanings, in their own words, in a log or journal. Encourage students to include a picture and example for the new word. Organizing the words by topic helps students make connections between the words (e.g., shape words, place value words, or decimal words). These logs provide reference during writing tasks, allowing students to find the words they need to express their ideas.

EXPLORING WORDS IN CONTEXT

Our repeated use of precise math words during lessons and demonstrations helps improve our students' math vocabularies in a natural way. As with any new language, however, students need opportunities to hear and speak it to make the words their own. Classroom activities that are interactive—requiring students to both talk and listen—help them develop vocabulary in a meaningful way. Students benefit from chances to explore new words and revisit ones that were previously introduced but may have been forgotten. Making the following a regular part of math instruction helps ensure a continued focus on the language of math:

- providing repeated exposure to words and meanings
- making connections between words.

Providing Repeated Exposure to Words and Meanings

Along with the advantages we've already discussed, having students talk with each other gives them many chances to hear and use new words. They benefit from hearing their classmates' ideas, as well as hearing the words their classmates have chosen to express those ideas. Students need to hear and see words used in context repeatedly to master them.

Lists of words related to the math topic being studied can be transformed into interactive vocabulary tasks. Place a set of words on cards or on the board, and then pose one of these quick and easy word activities to help students process and better understand the words.

1. Give a clue, then ask students to find the word that goes with your clue. Or ask students to come up with clues for words on the list and have classmates try to guess which word they are thinking of.
2. Ask students to find two words on the list that go together and to share their two words and explain the connection.
3. Ask students to illustrate a word on the list and then share their illustration with a partner.
4. Ask students to work with a partner to write a definition for a word on the list.
5. Have students work with partners to write riddles for one of the words and then pose the riddle to the class or create a flap book with the riddle on the front and the word inside.
6. Say a sentence, but omit a math word, and ask students to figure out which word is missing.
7. Give students a list of words from multiple topics, and ask them to find all of the words on the list that connect to one particular topic. This is a great review task.
8. Have students play What's My Word? Students choose a word card and then talk about the concept to a partner (without using the word) until the partner says the word.

See lists of key math vocabulary in each module of the grade-level books.

Students can also be exposed to new vocabulary through reading and writing exercises. As they read math textbooks, trade books, worksheets, and other materials, we can help students learn to use context clues as well as tools such as glossaries and diagrams to determine the meaning of words they encounter. Math materials can be excellent practice for students who are learning to identify and use expository text features such as an index, headings, or diagrams.

Making Connections Between Words

Making connections between different math terms helps students organize the ideas in their heads. Seeing connections between math terms is an indicator that students are making connections between the math ideas. Word webs and word sorts are examples of these types of word connection activities.

Word Webs

Students work in pairs or groups to brainstorm and record words related to a math term. If the designated word is *addition*, primary students might say *plus*, *add to*, *put together*, *more*, or *operation*. Older students might connect the word *decimal* to the related words *fractions*, *number*, *decimal point*, *money*, *tenths*, or *hundredths* (see Figure 4.10). After allowing students several minutes to work with a partner or team, the teacher records students' words on a class word web on the board or on chart paper. Then, the class discusses the various word connections, having students justify why each word belongs on the web by describing its relationship to the designated word or concept. The teacher adds illustrations or phrases to capture students' comments. When done, the word web looks much like a Math Talk chart, but the words and ideas have been generated by students. Although we focus on this as a vocabulary task, it is also a link to conceptual understanding of the math concept, strengthening students' understanding of the math ideas and the words that express those ideas. This is a valuable way to check prior knowledge before beginning a unit or to summarize words or concepts learned at the end of a unit.

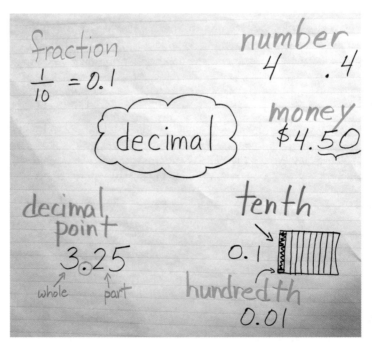

Figure 4.10 Students talk with partners to generate word associations, and then a class discussion highlights word meanings and the connections between the words.

Word Sorts

Students are given word cards with words or symbols related to a math topic. They are then asked to work with a team to sort the words into categories and decide on a title or label for each group of words based on their math meaning. The title should express how the words belong together (how they are alike or related). Teams are then asked to share and justify their groupings. There is no "correct" way to group the words (see Figures 4.11 and 4.12). Groupings should make sense for the words given.

In one such sort, students were given the following words and symbols to sort: *numerator, denominator, decimal, equivalent, divisor, whole, part, $\frac{1}{8}$, $\frac{8}{1}$, $\frac{8}{8}$, =, fraction, decimal point, tenths, hundredths, thousandths, 1.0, 0.1, 0.01*. Teams sorted them differently and a classroom discussion ensued as students shared and justified their thinking. One team (Figure 4.11) made groups of fraction words and decimal words, but also made groups they called *part* and *whole*, seeing 1.0, $\frac{8}{1}$, and $\frac{8}{8}$ as representations of wholes and 0.1, 0.01, and $\frac{1}{8}$ as connected to the concept of parts. If students are unable to find a group for a word, they are asked to justify why that word does not fit into any of their current groupings. This team was confused by *divisor* and the class had to discuss connections between that "division" word and the fraction concepts. As students share their groupings, discussions ensue and students gain a deeper understanding of math concepts while they are using important math words. Win-win!

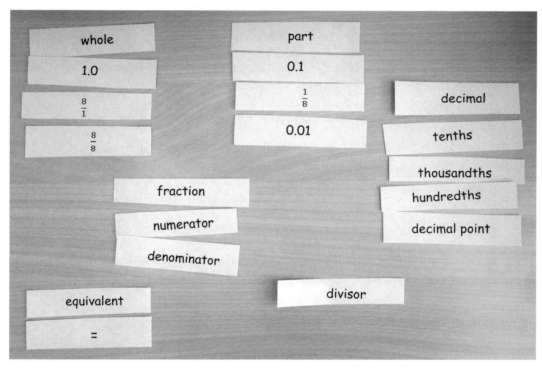

Figure 4.11 This team sorts the numbers based on whether they represent a part or a whole. Students place the decimal words together and the fraction words together, but cannot find a place for *divisor*.

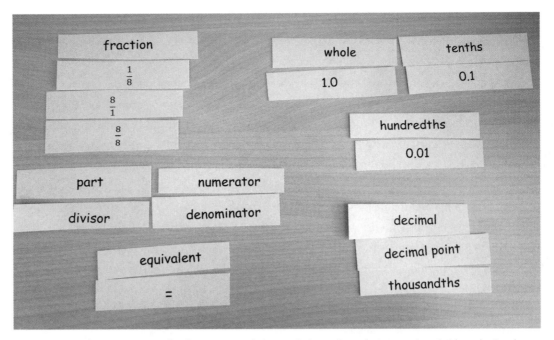

Figure 4.12 This team sorts the fractions and decimals based on their notation (with a decimal point versus with numerator over denominator). They notice a connection between *part* and *numerator* and *divisor* and *denominator* and are able to explain the connection to others in the class, helping some others to figure out a place in their sorting for *divisor*.

Challenge students to analyze and critique other teams' groupings.

- Are there words that could belong to more than one category?
- Is there a different way to think about the connections between the words?
    - Aren't decimals also fractions?
    - Could *divisor* go with *denominator*?
    - Could the numeric representations of 0.1 and 0.01 go with *tenths* and *hundredths*?

The goal is for deep thinking about the words and concepts and a productive discussion to extend students' understanding of the word meanings.

SETTING EXPECTATIONS FOR PRECISION

We introduce students to math words and give them repeated opportunities to explore the words and their meanings, but we must also expect students to use the words when they are talking or writing about math. By reminding them of important words for the content, phrasing questions to ask for precise language, and praising their use of specific words, we encourage them to incorporate these words into classroom discourse.

The posted Math Talk chart or word wall is an ongoing reminder of language that connects to the math being taught. Remind students that you expect them to use the chart to help them incorporate precise language into their discussions.

Mentioning vocabulary as you give directions for class, team, or partner conversations is another way to focus students on using the language meaningfully. You might ask students:

> *Tell your partner about how you found the sum. Can you use the word* regrouping *as you explain?*
>
> *Use the words* more than *to describe some data on the graph.*
>
> *Describe this geometric figure to your partner using the word* faces.
>
> *Tell your partner how you got the answer using the term* partial products.

When we circulate through the classroom during group work, we can listen for interesting vocabulary to share with the entire group (e.g., "In this group I heard someone say . . ." "Josiah and Hayley had an interesting way to describe . . ."). Listening for precise language as students work in teams and mentioning specific comments when debriefing with the class sends a clear message that precise language is important to you and to the class. And asking students to notice each other's word choices raises their awareness of the use of precise language.

> *What did Shontae say that clearly showed her understanding of place value?*
>
> *What did Makayla say that helped you understand her ideas about division?*
>
> *Joe used some very specific words to describe the shape. What words did he use that helped you get a picture of the shape in your head?*

Helping Students Communicate About Math

It is not easy for many of our students to put their mathematical thinking into words. If students answer in short phrases, misunderstand our expectations for what an appropriate response is, or lack precision in their responses, is math talk really achieving our goals? Helping our students learn to communicate mathematically allows our students to verbalize their ideas and strengthens classroom discussions.

Although thus far in this chapter we have focused on math talk, we now broaden our attention to include writing as well, because both are critical ways for students to express math ideas. Students learn to communicate effectively as they talk about and hear others talk about math ideas. They are able to hear their own thinking, restate their ideas when they don't come out the way they wanted, and hear others' ways of expressing those same ideas. They are able to revise and modify their talk on the spot, as they modify their thinking. But students also benefit from opportunities to express their ideas in writing.

As we write, we formalize ideas and find ways to express them clearly. We must recognize and organize our thoughts to put them in writing. Writing is hard, but when we are able to write about an idea, we have truly internalized the idea and made it our own. Consider providing students with many opportunities to write about their mathematical thinking.

Math journals are a common method for housing students' writing. These journals provide a spot for students to:

- brainstorm ideas
- draw models
- record predictions, observations, and conclusions about math investigations
- solve and reflect on math problems
- describe math concepts
- construct arguments
- explain procedures
- summarize the main points of a lesson or topic
- make connections between math ideas.

Although there are advantages to using bound journals, keeping writing together and allowing us to see progress across the school year, there are also advantages for having students write about math in other places. Because students often find writing difficult and sometimes tedious, balancing journal writing with opportunities to write on colored paper, folded paper, chart paper, or grid paper keeps students excited and engaged during writing tasks. It is not so much about where students write, but about keeping them writing and using that writing to extend and refine their math understandings.

TYPES OF TALK AND WRITING

As we are aware from our language arts lessons, talk and writing do not always look the same. We communicate for different purposes and teach our students that they can and should talk and write in different forms and with different goals depending on what they are talking or writing about. Some of the most frequent types of communication in mathematics, both in talk and in writing, include:

- describing or defining a math concept
- explaining how to do a process
- justifying an answer or method
- creating word problems
- comparing and contrasting strategies and concepts
- generalizing or drawing conclusions
- summarizing learning
- reflecting on learning.

Each of these supports students in a different way as they explore and make sense of mathematics. A look at each one highlights its value in the math classroom and suggests ways we can support students to more effectively communicate for that purpose.

Describing or Defining a Math Concept

Definitions and descriptions allow students to show what they know about math terms and concepts. Definitions may be brief, and descriptions often include examples, illustrations, or more detail.

Some ways to support students in describing concepts include:

- Remind students that they can use more than words to share their math ideas. Including pictures, numbers, and examples helps them more fully express their ideas.
- Focus students on important math vocabulary before they get started, asking them what words might be important to use as they describe an idea. Record a few of these vocabulary words on the board for students to consider.
- Model what a complete description looks like by writing some with students. You might start with having them write one of their own, then compare it with partners to get additional ideas. Pairs then share with the class, and then the class as a whole writes a final description as an example.
- At times, students may struggle with expressing what something is, but be able to say what it is not. Giving nonexamples can help students express their math understanding.

   Example: A square and a trapezoid are quadrilaterals.

   Nonexample: A triangle and a pentagon are not quadrilaterals.
- Using word boxes (see page 114) to describe a math concept pushes students to show their thinking in multiple ways. Sections might include: definition, example, nonexample, illustration.

Explaining How To Do a Process

How? is an important question in the math classroom. The study of mathematics is filled with procedures. When we ask students how they solved a problem, "I did it in my head" is not the response we are hoping for. When we ask students to tell us how they do a math procedure, we are pushing them to think about the steps they took and we are assessing whether those steps make sense. In this type of talk or writing, students are asked to indicate the steps and sequence for doing a process, such as how they figured out an answer based on data in a graph or how they solved a multistep problem. Here are some ideas to support this kind of communication.

- For writing tasks, have students try a numbered list to show the steps and order they used. Have them think about other writing they have seen in which a numbered list works (e.g., steps in recipes or steps on directions for assembling a toy). For many students, especially those who struggle with writing tasks, a numbered list is simpler than writing the procedure in a paragraph and just as effective for communicating their process.
- When talking about steps in a process, remind students of the power of sequence words like *first, next, then, finally* or *first, second, third.* Using these words indicates the order of our steps and helps others better understand what we are explaining.
- Consider a sequence chain graphic organizer for students who may need assistance isolating the steps they took to solve the problem. Students visualize each step as they

create their chain to show how they solved a problem or how they added two fractions with unlike denominators (see Figure 4.13).

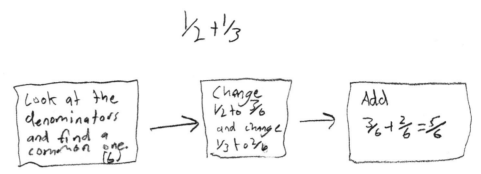

Figure 4.13 In a sequence chain, students visualize and record each step of the process.

- When explaining their methods for solving math problems, students often tell the computations they did, but don't link the computations to the problem. Linking the computations they did to the problem situation helps us determine whether they truly understand why they added or subtracted. Consider the following problem:

    There were 12 blue balloons and 18 red balloons. Colin tied the same number of balloons to each of 6 chairs. How many balloons were tied to each chair?

    Although one student responded, "I added 12 + 18 and then divided by 6 to get 5," another made connections to the problem situation to show us why she added and then divided (see Figure 4.14). If students give brief, computation-only explanations, help them understand your expectations by asking them for more details (Why did you add? What was the 30? Why did you divide by 6?). Explanations don't have to be long, but making connections to the problem and why the student chose the method they did makes them more precise.

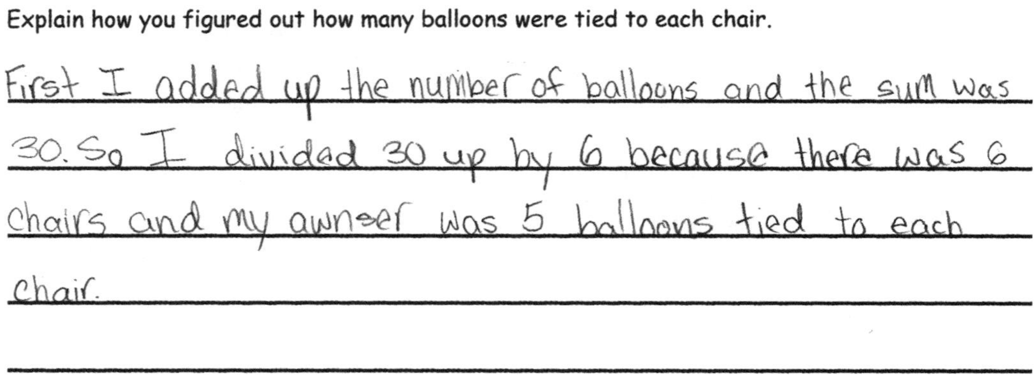

Explain how you figured out how many balloons were tied to each chair.

First I added up the number of balloons and the sum was 30. So I divided 30 up by 6 because there was 6 chairs and my awnser was 5 balloons tied to each chair.

Figure 4.14 This student mentions connections to the problem in her explanation, helping us feel more confident that she chose those operations because of her understanding of the problem situation.

- Encourage students to use words, pictures, and numbers to explain processes. Through computations, diagrams, and words, students' processes become clear as in Figure 4.15.
- Students sometimes lose track of the steps they took as they move through solving a problem, then when done, they simply mention the last thing they did (e.g., "I subtracted"). To help them identify their steps and construct more thorough responses, encourage them to go back to their work space after solving the problem and think about what they did, numbering each step. Then, as they explain verbally or in writing, they are able to tell what they did in order by looking at the numbers (as in Figure 4.16). The numbers guide their thinking and their talk and writing and allow them to give a more thorough response.

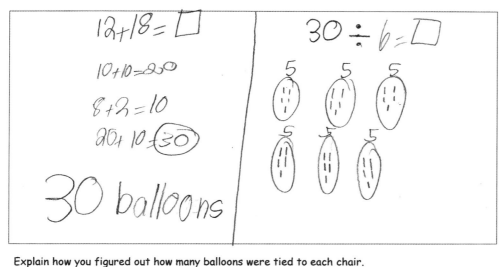

Explain how you figured out how many balloons were tied to each chair.

Well since there are 30 balloons and you need to tie the same amount on each chair. And I know 5×6=30 so 5 balloons on each chair.

Figure 4.15 This students shows her computations, creates a model, and explains her steps in words making her thinking evident.

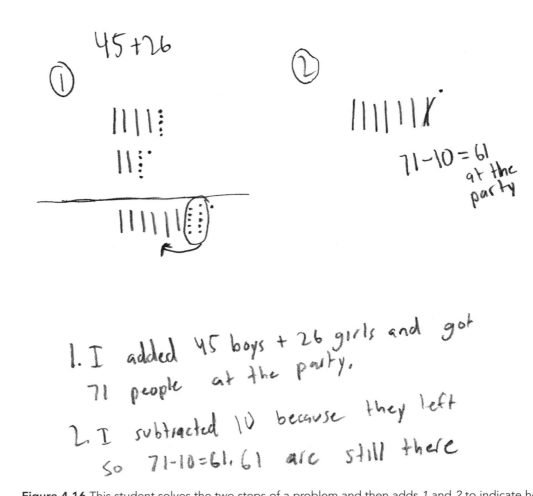

Figure 4.16 This student solves the two steps of a problem and then adds *1* and *2* to indicate her steps. She then writes a sentence to explain what she did in each step.

Justifying an Answer or Method

Justifying is about building arguments to defend, support, or prove that an answer is correct, a procedure is accurate, or a chosen process makes sense. We are asking students *Why?*

> *Why did you subtract?*
> *Why is $\frac{2}{3}$ more than $\frac{1}{2}$?*
> *Why is 0.5 the same as 0.50?*

Every day, our students should be asked to justify their mathematical thinking. They might be asked to defend an answer, defend how they solved a problem, defend a choice they made about selecting a tool, or defend a rule or generalization they suggested. And each time, they should be encouraged to prove their thinking with precision. "Justification is central to mathematics, and even young children cannot learn mathematics with understanding without engaging in justification" (Carpenter, Franke, and Levi 2003, 85).

In mathematics, constructing arguments is not about words only. Computations and models add to the strength of arguments. When building an argument for why $\frac{3}{8}$ is less than $\frac{3}{4}$, students might use math reasoning, models, or computations as follows:

MATH REASONING

Students might think about $\frac{1}{2}$ as a benchmark and explain "$\frac{3}{8}$ is less than $\frac{1}{2}$ because $\frac{4}{8}$ is $\frac{1}{2}$. $\frac{3}{4}$ is more than $\frac{1}{2}$ because $\frac{2}{4}$ is $\frac{1}{2}$. So if $\frac{3}{8}$ is less than $\frac{1}{2}$ and $\frac{3}{4}$ is more than $\frac{1}{2}$, then $\frac{3}{8}$ has to be less than $\frac{3}{4}$." Students might think about the meaning of denominators and explain "$\frac{3}{8}$ is less than $\frac{3}{4}$ because both of them are talking about 3 parts of the whole but in $\frac{3}{8}$ the whole was divided into 8 parts and those would be smaller than the parts in $\frac{3}{4}$ since that whole was only divided into 4 parts."

MODELS

Students might draw a number line and show $\frac{3}{4}$ and $\frac{3}{8}$ on the line or draw 2 rectangles of the same size, shading in $\frac{3}{4}$ on one and $\frac{3}{8}$ on the other as in Figure 4.17.

COMPUTATIONS

Students might find a common denominator to compare the fractions as in Figure 4.18.

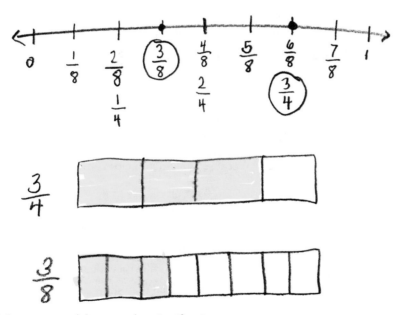

Figure 4.17 Accurate models strengthen justifications.

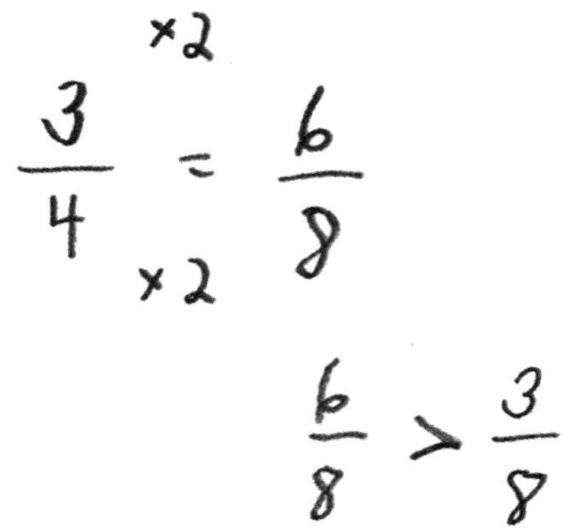

$$\frac{3}{4} \overset{\times 2}{\underset{\times 2}{=}} \frac{6}{8}$$

$$\frac{6}{8} > \frac{3}{8}$$

Figure 4.18 Applying an understanding of math computations strengthens justifications.

If a kindergarten student is asked which is greater, 5 or 2, and then asked to prove or defend their answer, they might use a model to show us that 5 cubes is more than 2 cubes, or draw a picture to show 5 balloons and 2 balloons, matching them to show that the 5 is more. They might show us the numbers on a number line or count to 5 to show us 5 comes after 2 so it is more than 2 because "every number is 1 more when you count." They are finding different ways to prove that 5 is more than 2.

Arguments are meant to be shared, inviting opportunities for students to critique ideas and debate approaches. When strong arguments are shared, students should be asked to identify what made the argument strong. When erroneous information is a part of arguments, students should challenge the information, modifying or correcting what is wrong. When unconvincing arguments are posed, students should work together to strengthen them. Debating math thinking through the building and critiquing of arguments strengthens students' understanding of mathematics.

To further strengthen students' ability to create arguments, try some of the following.

- Thinking about justifications as a "because" statement helps some students get started.

  I used division because . . .

  The answer is 45 because . . .

  0.5 is the same as 0.50 because . . .

- A good argument depends on precision. When asked to compare 314 and 297, many students simply said that 3 was more than 2, and while they likely understand that the hundreds digit had greater value and so that is what they should compare, they never said it, making the justification weak. The student in Figure 4.19 provides a bit more precision mentioning the hundreds place, but further challenging students to tell why they focused on those digits helps them recognize that precision helps strengthen their arguments and clarify their meaning.

Lots of Pennies

Annie and Ella counted the pennies in their banks.

Annie	Ella
314	297

Who has more pennies?

Annie has more pennies. I know she has more because _In the hundreds place Annie has 3 and Ella has 2 and 3 is higher than 2._

Figure 4.19 This student compares the 3 and 2 and mentions the hundreds place, but does not say why he chose to look at the hundreds digits. That insight would strengthen his argument.

- Agree or Disagree is a simple classroom activity that fits with any math topic. Pose a statement and ask students to agree or disagree with it and to justify their decision. Students might discuss the statement with partners and develop their arguments together, then share them with the class. This activity encourages students to listen to each other's arguments. Statements might include:

  7 + 3 and 4 + 6 are the only ways to make 10.

  5 tens and 3 ones is the same as 4 tens and 13 ones.

  9 is an even number.

  $2\frac{1}{2}$ feet are more than 32 inches.

  $\frac{3}{10} + \frac{4}{100} = \frac{7}{100}$.

  5.25 is greater than 5.4

  15 is a prime number.

Students used models and reasoning to build their arguments for the prompt "Bailey says $\frac{1}{3}$ is greater than $\frac{1}{2}$. Do you agree or disagree?" In Figure 4.20, the student disagrees and shows models and reasoning (although she incorrectly says that $\frac{1}{3}$ shades a quarter of the circle). In Figure 4.21, the student uses models and reasoning about the size of the denominator.

See the grade-level books for Agree or Disagree tasks specific to grade-level content.

Agree or (Disagree)

Bailey says $\frac{1}{3}$ is greater than $\frac{1}{2}$. Do you agree or disagree?
Use words, pictures, or numbers to show why.

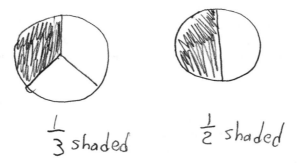

$\frac{1}{3}$ shaded $\frac{1}{2}$ shaded

NO. I disagree with Bailey.
This is why, If you look at
the picture carefully you will
see that $\frac{1}{2}$ shaded is greater.
It is greater because $\frac{1}{2}$ half
shades one whole side of the
circle. $\frac{1}{3}$ shades 1 quater of the
circle. Thats why I disagree.

Figure 4.20 This student uses models to clearly show that $\frac{1}{3}$ is less than $\frac{1}{2}$ and continues that $\frac{1}{2}$ "half shades" 1 whole and $\frac{1}{3}$ "shades 1 quarter of the circle." Feedback from classmates helped this student realize her mistake using the term *quarter* instead of *third*.

Agree or Disagree

Bailey says $\frac{1}{3}$ is greater than $\frac{1}{2}$. Do you agree or disagree?
Use words, pictures, or numbers to show why.

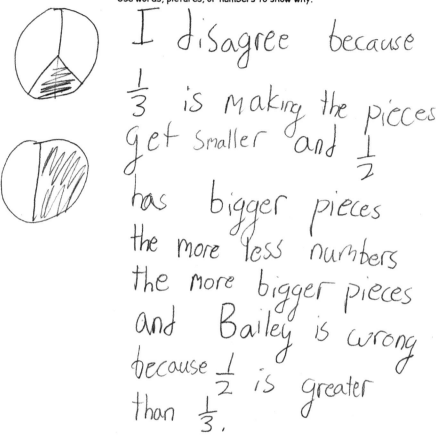

I disagree because $\frac{1}{3}$ is making the pieces get smaller and $\frac{1}{2}$ has bigger pieces the more less numbers the more bigger pieces and Bailey is wrong because $\frac{1}{2}$ is greater than $\frac{1}{3}$.

Figure 4.21 This student uses models to clearly compare the fractions and strengthen his argument and then adds reasoning about the size of the denominators indicating "the more less numbers, the more bigger pieces." Revoicing his idea, or asking for him to restate it, might help him find better words to express his thought that the smaller the denominator, the larger the parts.

- Eliminate It is another activity that helps students practice communicating their justifications. Four math words/numbers/models are presented to students (see Figures 4.22 and 4.23). Students then decide which one does not belong with the others and justify their decisions. Students might work with partners to build their arguments and then share them with the class to see if they can convince classmates of their thinking. There is often more than one possibility to eliminate, depending on student thinking.

See the grade-level books for Eliminate It tasks specific to grade-level content.

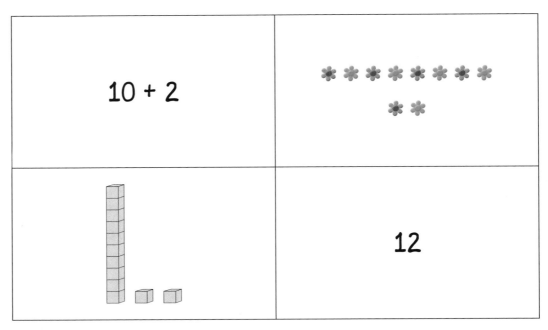

Figure 4.22 Primary students explore and discuss which of the numbers, expressions, or pictures does not belong with the others and justify why.

$.2 \times 10^4$	2,000
$.2 \times 10,000$	$.2 \times 1,000$

Figure 4.23 Fifth-grade students test their thinking about powers of 10 through an Eliminate It task.

- In Diagnose It, students are asked to perform the job of a doctor or a mechanic, both of whom diagnose problems and find ways to fix them. Students are given a math problem or computation that contains an error and asked to work with a partner or team to find the error and fix it. Students then justify their actions. For the following error, students explain why the answer is wrong (the student incorrectly subtracted 6 − 4 instead of 4 − 6).

$$\begin{array}{r} 194 \\ -76 \\ \hline 122 \end{array}$$

To fix this error, the student has to rename 194 as 1 hundred, 8 tens, and 14 ones and then subtract.

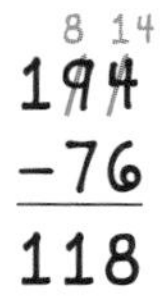

$$\begin{array}{r} {\scriptstyle 8 \;\; 14} \\ 1\cancel{9}\cancel{4} \\ -76 \\ \hline 118 \end{array}$$

Having students work together to diagnose problems highlights common errors and misconceptions and gives them practice justifying why what was done is incorrect or does not make sense mathematically.

Creating Word Problems

Writing word problems provides a critical link between doing math (computational skills) and understanding math (conceptual knowledge). Many students solve equations in a rote way, lacking the understanding of what the equations represent. Writing word problems to match equations challenges students to put a context to the abstract numbers and symbols of the equation. And it allows us to see if our students understand the equations they are solving.

A look at student-created word problems helps us assess students' understanding of operations (see Figures 4.24 and 4.25). The goal is for our students to be able to perform computations and understand what they are doing when they perform the operation.

For more on formative assessment, see Chapter 5.

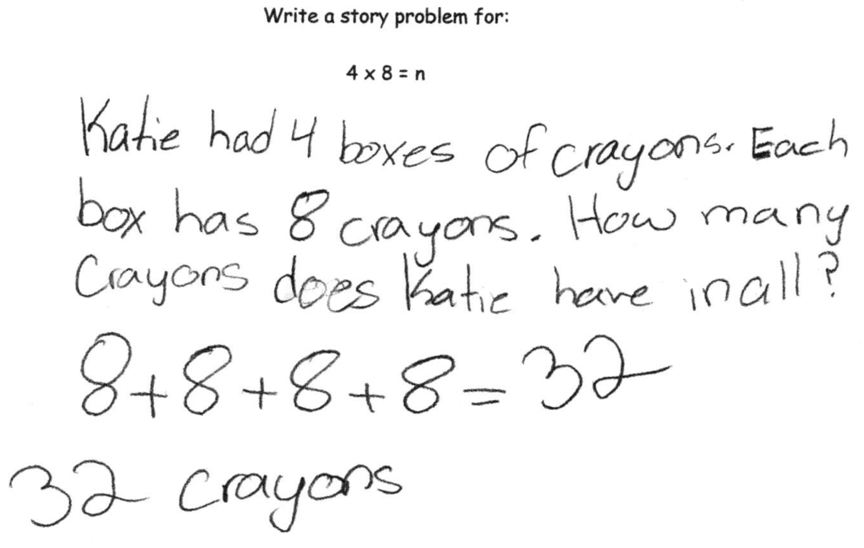

Write a story problem for:

4 x 8 = n

Katie had 4 boxes of crayons. Each box has 8 crayons. How many crayons does Katie have in all?

$8 + 8 + 8 + 8 = 32$

32 crayons

Figure 4.24 This student demonstrates an understanding of 4 × 8 = *n* by writing a context that makes sense with the equation.

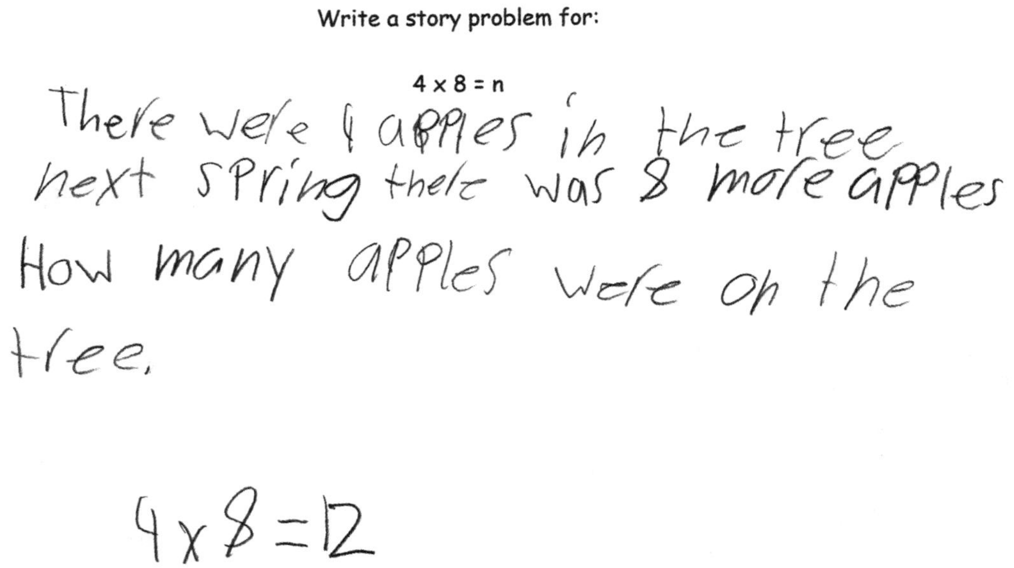

Write a story problem for:

$$4 \times 8 = n$$

There were 4 apples in the tree. next spring there was 8 more apples How many apples were on the tree.

$$4 \times 8 = 12$$

Figure 4.25 This word problem shows an addition scenario with 4 apples and then 8 more apples. This student needs additional discussions about what the numbers in a multiplication equation represent.

Following are some suggestions for working with students as they create word problems.

- Begin by writing some word problems with the class to model the thinking process. Put an equation on the board (e.g., 6 + 2 =___). Have students share ideas with partners as you pose questions to guide the creation of the word problem.

   What should we write about?

Students will share different ideas. Pick one for the day's problem—turtles, for instance.

   Where should our turtles be? (Swimming in the water.)

   How many turtles are swimming in the water? (6.) *How do you know?* (It is in our number sentence.)

   Talk to your partner about what could happen to our turtles that would show +2. (2 more go swimming.)

   So what is 6 + 2? (8.) *What is the 8 in our story?* (How many turtles were swimming altogether.)

This works at all levels. Students working with fractions might write stories for the equation $\frac{1}{2} + \frac{1}{3} = n$, for example.

   Look at the equation and tell me what we could be writing about.

Pick a possibility for the class demonstration—perhaps eating a granola bar.

   Who is eating this granola bar? (2 people: Lola and Cooper.)

   How could we show $\frac{1}{2} + \frac{1}{3}$? (One person could eat $\frac{1}{2}$ of it and the other could eat $\frac{1}{3}$ of it.)

   What would we be trying to find out? What is our question? (How much of the granola bar did they eat together?)

- Pose an equation and have students talk with a partner about a possible problem situation, writing the story together. Then, have partners share their problem and what each number in the equation represents.

  $3 \times 4 = n$

  Carter had 3 toy cars with 4 tires on each car. How many tires were there?

  3 is how many cars he had. 4 is how many tires are on each car. 12 is how many tires are on all of the cars.

- Tell students the answer is 35. Have partners write an equation in which 35 is the answer (e.g., $25 + 10 = 35$ or $39 - 4 = 35$) and then write a story to go with it. Have partners share with the class. Have students who built equations with the same operation look for similarities in the problem situations they wrote.

- Have students write a problem for one equation, then modify the problem as you adjust the equation.

  Pose $14 + 5 =$ __. There were 14 cookies on the plate. Mom put 5 more on the plate. How many were on the plate now?

  Pose $14 - 5 =$ __. There were 14 cookies on the plate. Mia ate 5. How many were on the plate now?

- Pose one of the following and challenge students to create story situations to match:

  Write a story problem that can be solved using multiplication (or addition, subtraction, or division).

  Write a word problem that must be solved in two steps.

  Write a word problem that can be solved using the formula A = l × w.

For more on making connections between equations and problem situations, see Chapter 2.

Comparing and Contrasting Strategies and Concepts

Comparing and contrasting concepts or strategies pushes students to think more deeply about them. When using counters to add $10 + 6$, primary students might compare counting all of the counters to counting on from 10 to find that both result in the same answer, but counting on is much quicker. Intermediate students might compare two strategies for solving a multiplication problem, finding that area models and partial products both show the same steps, but that partial products require less writing or that area models provide a better visual. Although students might be able to tell you that fractions and decimals are alike because both deal with parts and wholes, they may have difficulty verbalizing the specific differences between them (e.g., decimals as being base-ten fractions). Having to talk about how they are alike and different forces students to think more deeply about the concepts. By looking at similarities and differences between math concepts and processes in ways such as the following, students delve into their understanding of both and gain insights into the connections between them.

- Students might use graphic organizers like Venn diagrams or 2-column notes (see Figure 4.26) to record and organize their thoughts. Simply folding a paper in half and recording likenesses on one side and differences on the other can jump-start and give organization to students' thoughts.

Rectangles and Squares	
Ways They Are Alike	Ways They Are Different

Figure 4.26 2-column notes provide structure to students' recordings of likenesses and differences.

- When students are talking or writing about their comparisons, recognizing language that tells when things are alike (e.g., *both*, *also*, *same as*, *similar*) and different (e.g., *but*, *however*, *in contrast*) helps them express their ideas appropriately. Note that the word *similar* has a specific math meaning in geometry, which should be discussed with students to eliminate confusion when talking about similar figures.
- Provide regular opportunities for students to compare their strategies and approaches to solving problems (see Figure 4.27). Have them discuss what they did that was the same and what they did differently.

Figure 4.27 Frequent opportunities to compare their approaches helps students strengthen their skills at comparing and spurs insights about the math topic.

Generalizing or Drawing Conclusions

An important mathematical skill is the ability to analyze data and draw conclusions or generalizations based on that data. In Chapter 1, we talked about setting up investigations in which students gather, observe, and analyze data to draw insights from it. We talked about important questions including:

What do you notice?
Does it make sense?
Will that always happen?
What might you predict (for a related example)?
What is the rule?

In inquiry-based lessons that challenge students to observe, analyze, and generalize, we use talk and writing as a way for students to process the data, listen to others' ideas about the data, and ultimately, discover mathematical insights.

To help students with this key aspect of mathematical communication, try some of the following ideas.

- In this 2-column chart, students record observations on one side and then record their insights or conclusions on the other side. Students might simply fold a paper in half to take notes as their team discusses the data and then shares their conjectures or generalizations.

Observations	Conclusions

- Get students started with prompts to guide their thinking, like:
  I noticed . . .
  This is happening because . . .
  I wonder . . .
  I predict it will be . . . because . . .
  The rule is . . .

Summarizing Learning

Summarizing requires students to pinpoint key ideas. When we summarize, rather than telling everything, we focus on the most important things. As lesson closure, students might be asked to turn and tell partners the big ideas of the lesson. The whole class might then have a brief discussion to highlight those points. We might ask students to write short summaries as exit tickets or reflections. Summaries require students to distinguish important ideas from details and focus them on key learnings. We can help them with ideas such as the following.

- KWL charts are used to record what students know about a topic (K), what they wonder, or would like to know, about a topic (W), and what they learned about the topic (L). The first two parts (K-W) are discussed before lessons on the math topic and include prior knowledge from previous years or knowledge related to connected skills. The last part (L) is a summary of what was learned, including addressing those things students were wondering about before the lessons. The information on the chart could be used to write a summary of what was learned about the math topic.

- Have students work with partners or teams to develop a list of tips for students who have not yet learned a particular skill. The tips can be combined to make a class list for skills like adding 2-digit numbers, solving two-step problems, measuring volume, or adding fractions with unlike denominators. As students create their lists, they verbalize important ideas about the skill.

- Read *The Important Book* by Margaret Wise Brown. This primary book has a repeated sentence pattern that assists students in summarizing information. The book repeats the following writing format: "The important thing about _____ is _____."

    Then, a series of sentences provide details about the topic. Each section ends with, "but the important thing about _____ is _____."

    Students might use this format to write an "important book" about math topics. For example:

    The important thing about decimals is that they are fractions.

    Decimals are parts of a whole like fractions, but they have denominators that are multiples of ten, such as 10, 100, or 1,000.

    Each place in a decimal has a value like tenths, hundredths, and thousandths.

    Decimals have decimal points to separate the whole numbers and decimal parts, but the important thing about decimals is that they are fractions.

    You might adapt this to simply pose: "The most important thing is . . . Some other things are . . ."

Reflecting on Learning

Reflections can focus on content knowledge, mathematical connections, or students' attitudes about learning a particular math topic. Considering our students' reflections provides us with insights into their learning and helps us make informed decisions in our instruction. We might ask students to reflect on what was easy or hard about a particular lesson or topic, or list three new things they have learned, or identify things they still aren't sure about. An important question during problem-solving lessons is asking students to reflect on if and where they got stuck when solving the problem and how they got themselves unstuck.

Some ways to help students communicate their reflections might include the following:

- The 2-column note format offers a simple template for students to reflect on learning. Having the two headings reminds students to make comments on both ideas.

I Understand	My Questions

Some other possible headings include:

This Is Easy/This Is Hard

I Know This/I Am Confused About This

Skills I Know/Skills I Need to Practice

I've Got This!/I Need to Hear This Again

- Sentence starters are a great way to prompt reflections. Ask students to finish one of the following starters:

  I think it's easy to . . . I think it's hard to . . .

  During today's math class I felt . . .

  Today I made this mistake . . . I learned . . .

  I got stuck on the math problem when . . . I got unstuck by . . .

  I'm glad I can . . . I wish I could . . .

  I get confused when . . .

- For quick reflections, give each student a blank index card at the end of class. Have them label the sides 1 and 2. Pose a reflective prompt for each side (e.g., "On side 1, tell me something you feel confident about from today's lesson. On side 2, tell me something that you'd like to hear again." Or "On side 1, tell me something you know and on side 2, tell me a question you have."). The limited space on the card makes the exercise brief for students and allows us to quickly scan the cards for insights into students' thoughts and feelings.

- Students need to feel safe to express their frustrations and confusions. Having students share their difficulties in nonthreatening ways may be helpful. Having them write their ideas on exit slips at the end of class rather than sharing them verbally in class discussions where others can hear relieves anxiety and provides us with more honest reflections.

Hearing or reading students' reflections provides insights into who might be feeling confident, bored, or overwhelmed. As we become aware of their varied feelings about learning math and identify skills that may be easy for some but frustrating for others, we are reminded that students do not always learn math at the pace in which we teach and that their feelings about math impact their confidence and success.

Albert Einstein said: "If you can't explain it simply, you don't understand it well enough." Through experiences talking and writing in math class, our students explore ideas in more depth and develop the understanding needed to explain math concepts. Students may initially struggle to articulate their thoughts, but articulation improves as they sort out ideas and fine-tune their communication skills.

In addition, they show us their understandings and make evident their confusions and mis-understandings. Our ability to hear and read their thinking is an invaluable tool as we design lessons to improve that thinking. Listening to our students and reading what they have written is a way to get into their heads to determine what they know and what they still need to learn, and to help us figure out a way to move them from where they are to where we'd like them to be. We will explore that in detail in the next chapter.

 Scan this QR code or visit http://hein.pub/MathinPractice to see videos related to communicating about math and to access additional online resources (use keycode MIPGT).

Study Group Questions

1. Why have students talk about their math ideas?
2. How can we help students talk productively and precisely?
3. What is the relationship between vocabulary development and students' ability to communicate their mathematical thinking?
4. How can math vocabulary be developed in meaningful ways?
5. Which vocabulary development activities from other content areas might be used in the math classroom?
6. In what ways can talk and writing be integrated into daily math lessons?
7. How can we help students learn to communicate about math?
8. How does talking about math strengthen students' abilities to write about math?

Watch, Listen, Adjust

Letting Students Guide Our Teaching

One of the most dramatic changes in math teaching has been our shift in focus from teaching to learning. We have realized that the focus needs to be on students' learning and have reinterpreted our planning and teaching as ways to get them to their learning goals. We have begun to recognize that:

- Many students sit in the same lesson, but some get it and some don't.
- Some students need more time and exposure to certain skills and concepts to grasp them.
- Some students come to us without the foundational skills needed to grasp the new concept we are teaching.
- Some students come to us already knowing the skill we plan to teach.

It is of critical importance that we determine what our students know and what they may be struggling with, so we can make appropriate plans to help them.

Today, we question the traditional end-of-unit assessments and wonder why monitoring progress throughout teaching was not always an accepted practice. We realize that it is not about identifying who got a skill and who didn't at the end of a unit, but about helping everyone learn the skill.

Letting go of the control and letting our students guide our teaching means students, rather than a series of preplanned lessons, become the center of our planning. That does not mean that we are not focused on our standards, but simply that the way we get our students to mastery may look different for different students. To ensure our math teaching addresses the needs of our students, we recognize the importance of

- ongoing formative assessment to determine our students' strengths and needs
- differentiating instruction to address the varied needs of our students.

By focusing on our students' strengths and needs and letting their needs guide our math teaching, and by acknowledging that long-range plans will undoubtedly need revision and adjustments along the way, we are able to find ways to promote learning for all of our students.

Determining What Students Need: A Focus on Formative Assessment

In recent years, we have recognized the vital role assessment plays in instruction. Rather than assessment and instruction being viewed as separate—first we instruct and then we assess—we have acknowledged the interconnectedness of assessment and instruction. Formative assessment is not one event, but a collection of observations and tasks that help us determine what students know and how deeply they know it. Formative assessment helps us answer questions like the following:

- Who understands and who does not understand the concept?
- Who needs additional time and exposure to acquire the skill or understand the concept?
- What are a student's strengths and needs?
- What errors and misconceptions are occurring that need to be addressed?
- What feedback would help the students continue to grow?
- What adjustments should be made to instruction?
- How should students be grouped?
- How should instruction be modified for different students?

When we are able to determine what our students know, what they may be confused about, or where their understanding has broken down, we can adjust our teaching to build their skills and understanding. This is integral to our mission of teaching mathematics to all students. Formative assessment and effective instruction go hand in hand.

What the Research, Standards, and Experts Say About Formative Assessment

NCTM contends that effective teachers listen to their students' thoughts and explanations, observe them as they do math, and use that information to make instructional decisions (NCTM 2000). In *Principles to Actions* (NCTM 2014), one of NCTM's eight research-informed Mathematics Teaching Practices is "Elicit and use evidence of students' thinking," which emphasizes the importance of ongoing assessment of students' understanding of mathematics and the need to modify instruction to support our students' learning. Using assessment as an integral part of classroom practice is associated with improved student learning (Black and Wiliam 1998).

Formative assessment focuses on understanding as well as procedural skills (NCTM 2000). Evidence of how students think requires more than just whether students got the right or wrong answer (Crespo 2000). Effective formative assessment reveals students' thinking and uncovers their methods for solving math tasks. Strong assessment tasks provide opportunities for students to apply their knowledge and skills and transfer understanding to new situations (NCTM 1995).

Assessment and instruction should be consistent, having the same focus and similar formats (NCTM 1995). In fact, it should be difficult to distinguish when a teacher is assessing students' understanding, because it happens throughout instruction and looks and sounds like instruction. What a teacher does with the assessment data makes it unique. Formative assessment is used to modify instruction and improve student learning. Teachers might alter the next day's lesson plans to discuss specific misunderstandings, form small groups to provide additional exposure for students who may need it, or alter tasks to provide additional practice as needed.

Classroom instruction often yields unanticipated results. Through formative assessment, teachers are able to reflect on those results and reorganize their lesson planning as needed. "One of the complexities of mathematics teaching is that it must balance purposeful, planned classroom lessons with the ongoing decision making that inevitably occurs as teachers and students encounter unanticipated discoveries or difficulties that lead them into uncharted territory" (NCTM 2000, 18). Through formative assessment, we recognize when and how our teaching should be adjusted.

UNDERSTANDING THE INSTRUCTION/ASSESSMENT CYCLE

In the corresponding grade-level books, you will find activities labeled "Ideas for Instruction and Assessment." Most of the instructional activities can become formative assessments simply by how you observe, listen, analyze, or use the information gathered to modify your instruction.

Effective math teaching is a continual process of gathering information about how students are learning and then using it to adjust our teaching and improve student learning (Wiliam 2007). Math instruction is a cyclic process that begins with the end in mind. As we identify our learning goals (the critical skills or understandings we hope for), we design appropriate assessments to indicate whether students have reached the goal and select appropriate instructional activities to bring students to those outcomes. As we teach, we consistently check for understanding, provide feedback to students, and adjust our instruction. We continue moving our students toward those learning goals as we instruct, assess, provide feedback, and then instruct again (see Figure 5.1).

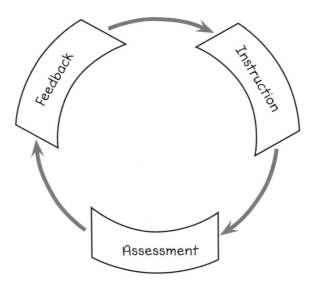

Figure 5.1 The process of teaching is cyclic as we instruct, assess, provide feedback, then adjust our teaching to continue moving our students toward the goals.

In most classrooms it is difficult to determine when assessment is happening because it is seamlessly woven into instruction. And feedback is recognized as an integral part of this process. Upcoming lessons are adjusted to clarify misconceptions, readdress topics, provide repeated practice, or allow for small-group interventions depending on what was learned through our assessment efforts. We do not stop teaching to assess; assessment and feedback simply become an integral part of the teaching process.

FORMATIVE ASSESSMENT OPTIONS

We have many choices when selecting a formative assessment task. Some assessment options give us a quick look at our students' understanding of a skill to allow us to make spontaneous decisions. Others allow us to look for depth of understanding or application of a skill. Do we want a general idea of whether the class is getting the concept to tell us if we should provide more examples or not, or do we want in-depth understanding about a particular student to determine the best way to help him? We select assessments based on the questions we'd like to answer (like the ones on page 140).

Formative assessment tasks can be formal (quizzes, writing prompts, performance tasks) or quite informal (listening to students as they turn and share their problem-solving methods, observing students as they work with manipulatives, posing exit tickets on which they show their work on one or two computations). Certainly different types of assessments yield different levels of information; some give us a general idea of who gets it and others provide us with an in-depth look at a student's skills and understandings. Following are some types of formative assessment tasks, including a discussion of their benefits as well as their limitations.

Every-Pupil Response Techniques

During instruction, it is helpful to do quick checks to be sure students are following the lesson and processing the ideas being shared. There are endless opportunities to conduct brief checks for understanding during class lessons. These might take the form of every-pupil response techniques (i.e., a thumbs up or thumbs down, operation pinch cards as mentioned in Chapter 1, or votes on an interactive board) in which every student is asked to simultaneously respond to a question. This assessment option gives a quick glimpse into students' thinking and may alter the course of our lesson by spurring on-the-spot decisions to provide additional examples or reexplain a concept. For that purpose, they are quite valuable, but we can sometimes be misled by seeing a thumbs up, later realizing that it was not an indicator of understanding but merely a fortunate guess. Following the thumbs up or active vote with partner discussions enhances this assessment option by allowing us to listen to our students' thinking. These tasks are easy to insert into our lessons to get a quick check, an indicator, of general understanding, but are not the best choice for assessing individual understanding.

Many teachers value the use of individual dry-erase boards on which students show computations or draw models and then turn them for the teacher to see. This quick look at student work allows us to determine if, and who, might benefit from additional time, examples, or support. Spontaneous small groups can be formed to give additional support to those who have been identified as needing it. In addition, the individual boards generate partner talk as students share their models and computations with those around them. And students love using them! It certainly does not feel like assessment to them.

Observing Students as They Work with Manipulatives

Observing students' work with manipulatives allows us to see what they know about a concept or skill. Their actions make their thinking visible. It becomes evident where misunderstandings occur when we watch kindergarten students explore solid shapes to see which roll, stack, or slide (see Figure 5.2), second graders compare numbers using base-ten blocks, or fourth graders draw a diagram to illustrate the area of a rectangular yard. A look at their representations provides us with data to assess our students' strengths and needs and allows us to adjust our instruction on the spot to address what we see.

For more on representations to show students' understanding, see Chapter 3.

Figure 5.2 The teacher watches and listens as this student explores the characteristics of solid shapes (e.g., they can roll or stack).

Listening to Our Students

Listening to students talk about their mathematical thinking provides us with invaluable assessment data. Verbal assessments can range from class discussions to listening to partner and team talk to individual diagnostic interviews.

Math is about thinking and thinking is invisible. To assess our students' thinking, we find ways to make it visible. Through open-ended questions and prompts that ask our students to explain, justify, and describe their answers and processes, we are able to assess their thinking, pinpoint their misunderstandings, and modify our instruction to meet their needs. The questions we discussed in Chapter 1 as instructional tools also provide us with invaluable assessment information. When students are asked to explain how they solved a problem, we are (1) helping them clarify their own thinking through verbalizing it, (2) generating class discussions with others who may have done it differently, and (3) identifying what they know or don't know. Our students' responses might

- give us confidence that students are internalizing important math ideas
- alert us to the need to review a concept with the whole class
- inform us of a small group of students who need additional support
- identify a student who has a misconception that must be addressed.

Class discussions can quickly resolve some misunderstandings as they occur; for others, further intervention may be needed.

All class discussions should serve as formative assessment. For students who do participate, we gain insights into their thinking. We may be able to identify both understanding and misunderstanding based on those students' comments, and we can determine the need for a whole-class review when no one is able to answer the question posed. But we are not able to assess students who have not shared a response, and we may not be able to assess the level of understanding when brief responses are given.

Thus, listening as our students collaborate with partners or groups provides us with invaluable data about each student. These assessments are informal, but require us to circulate and listen as our students work. This assessment doesn't happen from the front of the room. Having a place (a notebook or clipboard) to quickly record observations ensures that we remember important insights so we are able to act on them.

Individual student interviews give us in-depth and individualized assessments, allowing us to diagnose students' difficulties. Interviews may be indicated for specific students when we are unable to pinpoint their misunderstandings from previous written tasks or need them to interpret a piece of work. But it is also beneficial to periodically ask all students to share their thinking about a piece of work they produced, providing a unique opportunity to hear their thinking about math. In the primary grades, asking students to show us how they count by ones and tens, compare quantities, or decompose numbers gives us invaluable insights into these foundational skills (see Figure 5.3). Asking intermediate students to explain their computations with fractions or decimals or to justify their decisions and approaches when solving problems is equally beneficial.

Figure 5.3 This teacher observes and listens as the student demonstrates her counting skills. The teacher then probes to check her skills when additional counters are added to the row or when the counters are placed in different configurations.

Some teachers shy away from these interviews because of the perception that they are time-consuming, but although they do take time, they yield significant benefits. And conducting brief interviews, generally no more than a few minutes each, may prove to be a very efficient use of time. Scoring written tasks or reviewing math journals likely takes longer than simply asking students some directed questions about their thinking. And the answers to those questions allow us to consider, further question, and probe to find the reasons for students' confusions or misunderstandings. We might ask students to explain a model they drew, tell us why they chose a specific operation, or explain the steps they took to solve a problem.

So, when might we conduct these interviews? As students practice math skills, we have a perfect opportunity to both assess and remediate. As students practice, we might:

- circulate through the room to observe and listen as students work with partners
- work with a small group of students to provide additional support with the skill being practiced
- interview individual students to assess their understanding.

Circulating through the room is particularly helpful when new skills are introduced and we want to catch errors as students practice or apply the new skill, or as a means of identifying those students who may need additional support. Working with small groups is a useful option when we have confirmed that some students are able to work on their own, allowing us to focus on those who would benefit from additional exposure to the skill. And when students are involved in meaningful individual or partner practice, conducting interviews is a sound option because it allows us to uncover the roots to why a particular student may be struggling or to conduct routine checks for understanding to be sure that students have the mathematical thinking that underlies the skill they are practicing. Finding just the right time to conduct interviews, while others are actively involved in math tasks, allows us to capitalize on this highly effective assessment option.

Brief Written Tasks

Through brief open-ended tasks, we gain insight into students' thinking. These tasks require students to do some math and may ask them to explain their thinking. We might ask students to show us 256 in varied ways (e.g., standard form, word form, expanded form, or models). We might ask them to show us three quadrilaterals and tell us something they know about quadrilaterals. We might pose a statement and ask them if they agree or disagree and to prove their thinking (see Figure 5.4). We might ask them to solve one or two computations (e.g., $10 - 5 = \_\_\_$, $45 - 29 = \_\_\_$, or $4.56 - 2.7 = n$), including a model to show their work, allowing us to analyze their work to see if their understandings, solutions, and processes are reasonable.

These tasks are brief and can be directed specifically to a key learning goal (see Figure 5.5). The brevity of the task allows us to check these in a timely way and make adjustments in our plans for the following day's lesson, as well as give immediate student feedback to correct errors or clear up confusions. But, because these are open-ended tasks, it is difficult to assess responses that are brief or unclear. Follow-up interviews may be needed to interpret some students' responses (see Figures 5.6 and 5.7). Because formative assessment happens during instruction, we don't expect to see all perfect papers; on the contrary, we want to be able to identify students' errors and misunderstandings so we are able to address them.

Rita says $\frac{1}{3}$ is greater than $\frac{1}{2}$. Do you agree or disagree? Use words, pictures, or numbers to show why.

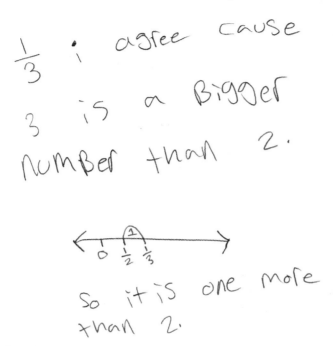

$\frac{1}{3}$: agree cause 3 is a Bigger number than 2.

So it is one more than 2.

Figure 5.4 This student shows a lack of understanding about what the fractions represent, including a misunderstanding of denominators. Additional discussions about the meaning of denominators are indicated, as well as added exposure to fraction number lines.

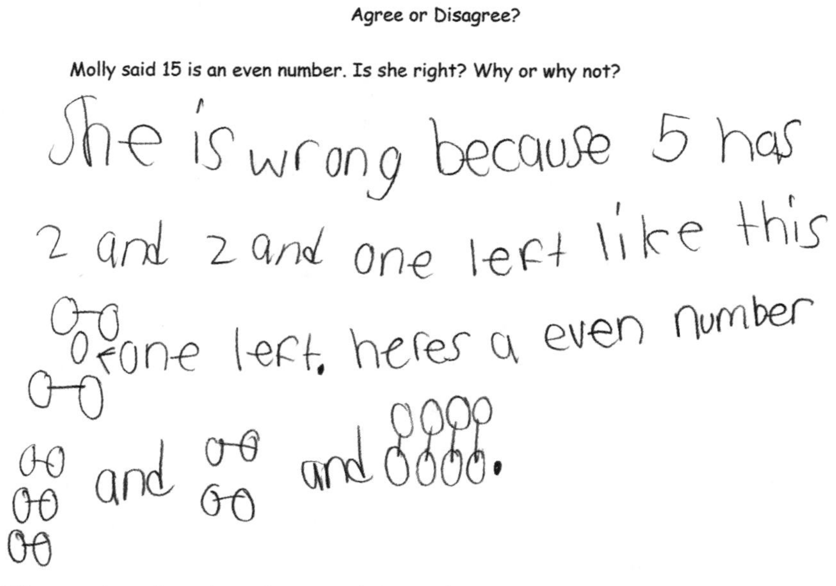

Agree or Disagree?

Molly said 15 is an even number. Is she right? Why or why not?

She is wrong because 5 has 2 and 2 and one left like this one left. heres a even number

and and .

Figure 5.5 This student describes the "one left" as the reason 15 is not an even number and then creates several models to show the matching of twos that occurs in even numbers.

Molly said 15 is an even number. Is she right? Why or why not?

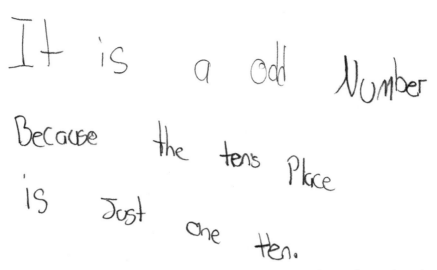

Figure 5.6 Further clarification is needed to understand why the student is focused on the tens digit. Does he understand that 1 is an odd number, but is focusing on the tens digit rather than the ones digit? The written work helps us identify that a misunderstanding is occurring, but a brief interview with this student would yield helpful information about his misunderstanding.

Agree or Disagree?

Molly said 15 is an even number. Is she right? Why or why not?

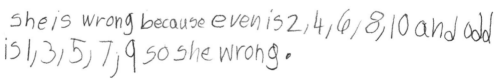

Figure 5.7 This student believes he has answered the question, but his response leaves us wondering if he really understands what an even number is. A follow-up interview, in which we ask him to tell us what an odd number is, allows us to assess if he doesn't know or just didn't include it in his writing.

These assessments might take the form of exit tickets or journal writing at the end of a lesson. They could be done on individual dry-erase boards during classroom tasks, but that would require us to assess as we are teaching or circulating through the room as students work, jotting down observations so we remember both the errors and who might be experiencing difficulty. Having students record these tasks on paper allows us to collect them and review them for the following day. And the brevity of the tasks help us quickly review a class set of papers, pinpoint errors, and address those errors in a timely way, a necessity when we are trying to quickly identify misunderstandings so they can be immediately addressed.

Problem-Based Tasks

Our standards focus on the expectation that our students are able to understand and apply math skills. Providing problem-based assessments allows us to determine not only if students know how to do a math skill, but if they know when and how to apply the skill to a problem situation. These problem-based assessments might take the form of word problems or might be assignments in which students have to perform a task (e.g., select food items for a dinner based on a restaurant menu, determine a schedule for a trip to the zoo based on the times of animal feedings, design a new playground using their understanding of area, or plan a trip and determine mileage and travel costs). As in all of our assessment tasks, we look at more than answers as we analyze their problem solving. For each problem task, we are able to gain insights about

- their problem-solving skills:
  - Did they know which operation or math skill made sense to solve the problem or perform the task?
  - Could they build an equation to help them with the task?
  - Did they demonstrate perseverance if they got stuck?
  - Were they able to use alternate strategies to continue the process?
  - Is their answer reasonable for the problem situation?
- their computational skills:
  - Were they able to correctly perform the computational task and arrive at the correct answer?
- their understanding of math concepts:
  - Were they able to apply their understanding of place value, time, money, or other math concepts as needed?
  - Were they able to select appropriate formulas (e.g., to find area, perimeter, volume)?
- their communication skills:
  - Were they able to effectively model the problem?
  - Were they able to explain how they solved the problem or justify their method or solution?

Problem-based tasks require our students to put together varied skills to reach a solution or perform a task (see Figure 5.8). By posing problem-based tasks that include prompts for students to explain their thinking, we are able to better pinpoint where in the process they may need additional support. The scoring of these problem-based tasks takes more time and is generally scored with a rubric because the tasks incorporate multiple skills. For students with very weak skills, the tasks can feel overwhelming and may need to be modified to provide us with usable data. See page 167 for ideas on modifying math tasks for readability, length, or complexity of data.

A variety of problem-based tasks are available in the online resources and throughout the grade-level books.

Blake made 1 gallon of lemonade for her lemonade stand. She sold $\frac{3}{4}$ gallon of the lemonade on Monday. On Tuesday she sold $\frac{1}{2}$ of what was left. How much did she sell on Tuesday?

Draw a diagram and show any equations you used to solve the problem.

Explain how you figured out how much lemonade she sold on Tuesday.

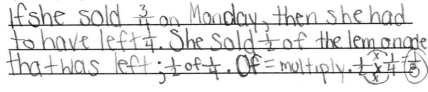

Figure 5.8 This student demonstrates through her model, computations, and explanation that she understands the problem, can apply the correct math to the situation, and can effectively find the solution. She is able to clearly communicate how she solved it.

A Word on Rubrics

Rubrics are not about determining right or wrong. They help us figure out where our students are on a continuum from "struggling with every part of the task" to "can put it all together." Between those two ends of the spectrum is a range of partially demonstrated skills. Rubrics help us determine which skills students are able to demonstrate and which skills need further development.

Rubrics are beneficial for guiding and evaluating student work, but reap the greatest benefits when they are shared with our students prior to beginning the task. As we design rubrics, we are focused on identifying the critical outcomes we expect. When reviewed with students prior to the assignment, rubrics allow students to identify the criteria on which their work will be judged. During the task, rubrics guide students as they work, serving as a reminder of the critical components of the task. After completing the task, rubrics allow us to evaluate a student's performance based on specific criteria rather than comparisons to others' work. Rubrics also serve as a guide for peer review and self evaluation.

Holistic rubrics analyze our students' abilities to put it all *together* to perform a task. In designing a rubric for a problem-solving task, the outcomes that are important to you may include the following:

- the ability to choose a reasonable strategy (one that gets the student to the answer)
- the ability to find the correct answer
- the ability to model the problem, explain how the problem was solved, or justify the answer (depending on the specific task).

The outcomes represent the students' problem-solving skills, computation skills, and communication skills. If these outcomes are deemed important, all three should be a part of the scoring rubric. One possible set of scoring points might be:

4 – The strategy used to solve the problem is appropriate.
    The answer is correct and properly labeled based on the problem.
    The explanation is thorough (including all steps) and precise (giving specific details of what was done) and uses key math vocabulary.

To score a 4, all of these criteria must be met.

3 – The strategy used to solve the problem is appropriate.
    The answer is correct, or contains only minor errors.
    The explanation is understandable, but may lack details.

The score of 3 allows for some minor computation errors and some lack of clarity in the explanation, but requires students to use a reasonable strategy.

2 – The strategy used to solve the problem is appropriate.
    The student calculated a correct answer, but the explanation may be difficult to understand; or the answer was incorrect, but the student was able to adequately explain the strategy used.

The score of 2 also requires students to use a reasonable strategy (a priority for the problem-solving task), but students may have gotten an incorrect answer or been unable to explain their thinking.

1 – The student did not use an appropriate strategy.
    The answer is incorrect.
    The explanation is incorrect or unclear.

If students are unable to apply a reasonable strategy, the foundation of problem solving, they score a 1.

continues

0 –   The page is blank/the student made no attempt.

A score of 0 is for the student who does not attempt the task. To be a problem solver, students have to be willing to take a risk and try. In this rubric, students get 1 point simply by trying a strategy.

Tips for Using Rubrics

Use student-friendly language.

- If the students can't understand the rubric, it will be ineffective to guide instruction, reflection, and assessment.

Use the rubrics with your students.

- Students should be familiar with and understand the rubric. Use it as a conversation piece before tasks, during lessons, and during post-task student conferences.

Don't overwhelm with too much information.

- You want the rubric to be understandable and organized, but not overwhelming. Although you may identify 10 things you would like to see, pick the most important criteria for that particular task so students can focus on those points.

Consider some common rubrics and templates.

- Although some tasks may require a specifically designed rubric, other tasks may be able to fit a more generic scoring tool, such as the problem-solving rubric above.
- Templates to develop classroom rubrics and samples of math rubrics are available on a variety of online sites, like Rubistar (http://rubistar.4teachers.org) and Exemplars (www.exemplars.com/resources/rubrics/math-rubrics). Beginning with these templates and then modifying them to meet your needs helps streamline the development process.

Tests and Quizzes

Certainly there is a place in the assessment process for tests and quizzes, but the way in which we use the results indicates whether or not they are a part of the *formative* assessment process. If the results are used solely to designate a grade, they are not formative assessment. If, however, the results are analyzed to determine next steps for the teacher, or to provide specific feedback to a student on how to improve her understanding or skills, they are a part of this instruction/assessment cycle. Consider, however, making tests or quizzes multiformatted, possibly having some computation-only tasks and some constructed-response items.

- Decrease the amount of computations on tests and quizzes to allow you to add writing components that give greater insight into students' thinking.

- For multiple-choice formats, have students justify their choice, allowing you to determine if it was a guess or an informed choice.
- Allow for more than one possible answer on a multiple-choice format so students have to think more deeply about each possible response.
- Encourage students to "show their work" to help you determine why an answer might be wrong or to convince you that their right answer was based on understanding.

Gathering data to improve learning is the goal of formative assessment. Any format that provides us with insights about our students' learning helps us gain a more balanced picture of their strengths and needs.

Formative assessment is often a matter of drilling down for more specific data. We may try one assessment format and get some data, but need more specific data on some or all students, so we try something else. Formative assessment is not one task, it is a collection of tasks that give us ongoing evidence about what our students know and can do. We continue the instruction/assessment cycle as we collect data, readjust instruction, gather more data, and readjust instruction again.

Developing Common Assessments

It is an increasingly common practice for teachers at a grade level to design common assessment tasks. The process of designing these tasks as a team can be as beneficial as utilizing the actual tasks. As we refer to our math standards and articulate what we want students to be able to know and do, we become more familiar with our standards and more tuned in to how our students can demonstrate their skills and knowledge for us. Grade-level teams ask themselves:

- What do we want our students to know and be able to do?
- What evidence tells us this student has reached that learning goal?
- What can we do to get our students there?

Learning goals are included for all skills in the grade-level books.

Identifying the learning goal and designing an appropriate assessment task come first, followed by discussions about how to organize instruction to get our students to the learning targets.

Administering common assessments also allows us to share our experiences and discuss our observations of students with colleagues. When students in one class show understanding, we are able to discuss the specific classroom activities that may have benefited them. When students in different classrooms struggle with similar concepts, we can brainstorm intervention ideas, share resources, and discuss possible approaches.

USING ASSESSMENT DATA

A critical component of formative assessment is that we *do something* as a result of the evidence we gather (Wiliam 2007).

Adjusting Instruction

It is rare that formative assessment tasks show that the whole class needs assistance with a skill, but should that happen, reteaching the skill or revisiting a concept is essential. It is more likely that formative assessment results in small-group or individual assistance.

Our actions might include any of the following:

- Reteach a concept to the class in a new way (not restating what we already said) and then gather data again.
- Continue to revisit a concept/skill for the next few days or weeks with a brief example or quick discussion each day.
- Provide specific feedback to the whole class, small group, or individual student to clarify a misconception.
- Create flexible groups to revisit the skill at different levels.
- Work with a small group for reteaching or enrichment.
- Conference with an individual student to gather more diagnostic data about his understanding.

The only time we would not take an action based on our formative assessment is when every student hit the learning target. Otherwise, the point of formative assessment is to readjust our instruction to keep students moving toward the goal. Tell students when you are reteaching a lesson and why ("I noticed on your exit tickets that . . ."). Let students in a small group know why you have brought them together. Talk about a misconception that surfaced during an assessment. Let your students know their strengths and needs. Feedback to students is a part of this process. (We will discuss ways to modify instruction to meet our students' needs later in this chapter.)

Sharing Feedback with Students

Providing feedback is essential to helping our students improve their learning. Feedback has been shown to be one of the most significant activities a teacher can engage in to improve student achievement. Using assessment data to provide feedback to students allows them to figure out what they need to do to close the gap between their current performance and their learning goals (Hattie 2008). In their *Assessment Standards for School Mathematics*, NCTM asserts "If students are to function as independent learners, they must reflect on their progress, understand what they know and can do, be confident in their learning, and ascertain what they have yet to learn" (1995, 14).

A common misconception is that giving students a graded paper with incorrect items marked is feedback. If feedback is a means to improve instruction, is that true? Research has supported the importance of quality feedback, but what constitutes quality feedback?

TIMELINESS

Feedback must be timely if it is to impact student learning. If exit slips are reviewed a week after we give them, how does that help our students? Have they practiced using the same error for the past week? Is the feedback still relevant to them? Immediately addressing misconceptions and errors is critical.

AMOUNT

Feedback must be a manageable amount. If a student has multiple errors/misunderstandings, select the most critical ones first. There is nothing more dejecting than a paper filled with red marks. Provide enough feedback to help, but not overwhelm, students. Be sure that your comments refer to strengths as well as errors. Positive feedback motivates students.

AUDIENCE

To be effective, feedback needs to be directed to the right audience. Who will benefit from your feedback? Does the whole class need to hear it, a small group, or just one student?

METHOD

Feedback can be given orally, in writing, or through demonstrations. What is the most effective way to relay your feedback?

- Oral feedback allows students to hear it right away and allows you to clarify and further assess their understanding through questions and discussions. This option is particularly helpful when the feedback is difficult to put into writing or students don't read well.
- Written feedback provides students with a permanent copy of your comments, so they can refer back to them if needed. And written feedback allows parents to see your comments and suggestions.
- Demonstration feedback, modeling ideas and processes, provides both verbal and visual cues, so students can see and hear what it looks like. This might include demonstrating a skill with manipulatives or showing a computation, highlighting each step in a different color, emphasizing those steps that the students struggled with.

OBJECTIVITY

Feedback should be objective and focused on skills. Using rubrics to guide feedback is a way to keep it objective because in rubrics students see the criteria used to judge their work. Before the task, reviewing the rubric helps students focus on what they need to do. During the task, referring back to the rubric keeps them focused and on task. After the task is complete, the rubric allows them to review their own work and allows others to review it in a nonjudgmental, objective way.

PRECISION

Many traditional teacher comments ("Great job," "Incomplete," "Sloppy," and so on) are useless in improving performance. Fine-tune the feedback you provide to students by making it specific (see Figure 5.9).

What Was Said	What Was Meant
"Incomplete."	"You answered the first part of the problem (how many blocks Jan had), but not the second part to find the total for both Jan and John."
"Very thorough."	"You gave me all three things I asked for: the answer, a model, and an explanation."
"Nice work."	"Your answer is correct and I can follow exactly what you did because of your step-by-step explanation of how you solved the problem. I like the way you labeled the steps 1, 2, 3 . . ."
"Put more effort into your work."	"I am only seeing an answer when I asked you to show your work. I need to see the computations that got you to that answer."
"Defend it."	"Why did you decide to multiply? Can you prove to me that multiplying was a good decision?"
"Nice perseverance."	"I like the way you tried a different strategy (making a table) when the first thing you tried did not work. I'm so glad you didn't give up!"
"Sloppy work."	"I don't understand your diagram. Label the dimensions and show your equation so I am able to see what you have done."

Figure 5.9 Precise feedback allows students to identify exactly what they did that was valued and exactly what they need to do to improve their work.

INVOLVING STUDENTS IN THE ASSESSMENT PROCESS

Students should have an active role in the formative assessment process. When errors or misconceptions are detected, student actions are important. Although we may share our feedback, students must be able to understand and internalize that feedback and have the opportunity to respond to it in some way. Students might be asked to redo a task, write about their understanding, solve a similar problem, or explain to us how they would perform a task. The goal is not that all students have to do it right on the first try; it is that they can get it right after feedback, reflection, and practice.

Involving students in self-assessment helps to focus them on the learning targets. You might share a checklist of what you expect to see in a response and have them look for evidence that they met the outcomes (e.g., "I multiplied accurately and got the correct product, I included an area model to show my work, and I told why multiplication made sense for this problem"). Consider brief conferences with students in which you review a piece of work together and ask them to tell you what they know and still need to work on. Have students collect samples of their math work to create a math portfolio, with reflections on each piece of work (e.g., "I did this well . . . Next time, I will . . ."). Have students frequently look back through portfolio samples, or math journal entries, to note the progress they have made throughout the year. Or have them consider their understanding about a topic and write reflections (e.g., "I know . . . I still need help with . . ."). Our students are an integral part of the instruction/assessment cycle.

The formative assessment process allows us to see what our students know and are able to do and to identify where they need additional support. Implicit in the formative assessment process is that it is used to guide our instruction.

Responding to What Students Need: A Focus on Teaching Mathematics to All Students

As we uncover misconceptions, discover missing foundational skills, or recognize mastery of skills, we are challenged to let that data guide our instructional approaches. In many cases, we find that the needs we uncover are varied, and we are challenged to find ways to help all of our students understand the math we are teaching.

In a differentiated classroom, we see whole-class instruction and teacher-led small groups, as well as students working independently, with partners or teams, or exploring math ideas at centers. We see students modeling with concrete materials, drawing math representations, talking about math, and using abstract methods. We see teachers who modify tasks to pinpoint students' needs. In a differentiated classroom, we find teachers who are willing to adapt and adjust their teaching methods and tasks to help all students find success.

What the Research, Standards, and Experts Say About Meeting the Needs of Varied Learners

In *Principles to Actions*, NCTM (2014) identifies "access and equity" as one of its guiding principles for school mathematics, noting that a high-quality mathematics program ensures that there are high expectations for all of its students and that they all receive the assistance and resources needed to maximize their learning. In their *Position Statement on Access and*

Equity in Mathematics Education, NCTM (2014) states that achieving access and equity requires that students be taught by skilled teachers who differentiate instruction as needed including allowing adequate time for students to learn, monitoring students' progress, making needed accommodations, and offering remediation and extensions as appropriate. In *It's Time*, The National Council of Supervisors of Mathematics (2014) recommended that "various learning experiences are provided that are appropriate for the range of learners in the classroom (i.e., differentiation by content, process, and/or product)" (69).

Tomlinson (2014) highlights three ways that teachers generally differentiate instruction: by adjusting the content (what students learn), by adjusting the process (how students learn), or by adjusting the product (how students demonstrate what they learn). Inherent in this differentiation process are many research-based strategies including the use of ongoing assessment, the significance of teaching to students' needs, and the benefits of flexible grouping for instruction. We've already discussed the first of these; in the rest of this chapter, we'll examine the other two.

MEETING OUR STUDENTS' NEEDS

Our classrooms are filled with diverse learners; some are ready to be challenged with complex tasks and others need ongoing support, encouragement, and remediation. Our goal is to help all of them learn mathematics.

Many students long for a challenge. Rather than moving them to content from the next grade level, we now choose to enrich with depth, posing problems, puzzles, and challenges that extend their thinking about the math topics we are studying. By modifying math tasks, allowing them to work in like-ability teams, challenging them in small-group lessons, and creating centers with leveled tasks, we enrich their experiences and extend their thinking.

Other students require modifications for different reasons. To build their confidence, relieve their anxiety, and bolster their foundational skills, we offer remediation through small-group lessons that revisit previously taught skills, modified tasks that fit their abilities, adjusted center tasks that provide meaningful practice, and additional time to explore and learn math.

Our students come to us with different prior knowledge, learn at different rates, and process knowledge in different ways. Our goal is to help them all learn mathematics. As we reflect on our math teaching, we consider the many ways we can help them build a strong foundation during the K–5 years, setting them up for success as they move to the middle grades and endless possibilities for their future.

Differentiated instruction is not individualized instruction, but rather a process of adjusting classroom practices to provide students with varied ways to acquire content, process ideas, and express their understandings. We have a wide range of options for meeting the varied needs of our students:

1. varying our teaching techniques—teaching in different ways to be sure that all students can access the ideas
2. providing varied instructional formats—varying our teaching formats from whole class to small group to partners to centers to provide different levels of support
3. modifying math tasks—ensuring that our tasks are challenging but doable, based on our students' needs.

It is daunting to think about meeting the needs of so many learners, but differentiation is about recognizing options that make our teaching more effective and focused on our students' needs.

Varying Our Teaching Practices

How did you learn mathematics? In the past, math was taught in the same way day after day. If you thrived on hearing the steps for doing a procedure, then practicing quietly with paper-and-pencil tasks until you had memorized those steps, it is likely that you were successful in math class. That teaching practice worked for many, but did it work for all? Clearly not, because many adults believe they can't do math and reminisce about feeling lost during math lessons. What if you needed to visualize ideas, wanted to talk about your thinking, or longed to investigate concepts to figure out why they worked? Today we recognize that when it comes to instructional strategies, one size does not fit all. We wonder how many more students might have developed math abilities and confidence if the concepts had been presented in different ways so that many types of learners could access the ideas.

Strong and colleagues (2004) identified four mathematics learning styles: mastery, understanding, interpersonal, and self-expressive. The styles suggest that students favor one of the following four approaches for learning mathematics: step-by-step computations, reasoning with explanations and proof, applications with group discussions and connections to real life, and visualization and exploration. Their work suggests that designing lessons that incorporate procedural, conceptual, contextual, and investigative styles benefits the varied learners in our classrooms. Varying the ways in which we ask students to explore math ideas ensures that all students have opportunities to think about the skills and concepts in ways that make sense to them.

Consider second graders exploring the comparison of two 3-digit numbers. Through a variety of tasks, students are able to engage in experiences that span varied learning styles from step-by-step approaches to reasoning to group discussions to visual/explorations as in the following examples:

- Students explore the concept in a step-by-step approach using base-ten blocks (visual materials) as they build and compare numbers.

- Students work with partners or groups to compare two numbers using concrete materials and practice recording their ideas using the symbols >, <, =.

- Teams investigate to find a rule for comparing 3-digit numbers by building and comparing numbers, recording which is greater, and then discussing their observations of the digits, employing their reasoning skills to generate a rule and prove that the rule makes sense.
- Students work in pairs or alone on real-world problems in which numbers must be compared, followed by justifications of their solutions.
- Students engage with partners at a math center and use their reasoning skills to compare numbers without manipulatives.

Balancing our instruction with step-by-step approaches, reasoning with explanations and proof, applications with group discussions and connections to real life, and visualization and exploration ensures that all students are able to engage with the content. As we vary our teaching strategies, we feel confident that each child has opportunities to experience the concept in a way that makes sense to her. In addition, varying our teaching draws students in to math lessons. When students are engaged, they learn. We shift the focus from the monotony of workbook pages, all too often a staple in math classrooms, to a wealth of engaging tasks that have our students exploring math ideas from different perspectives. Math class should be concrete, visual, interactive, and reflective. Varying our instruction helps all students become active learners of mathematics.

And for all students, we revisit math concepts and skills throughout the year. In Chapter 2, we discussed the importance of content progressions as we build on skills from year to year. We know that learning about shapes or fractions or division in November, without revisiting those ideas frequently throughout the year, is likely not to result in retention and will surely impact our ability to build on those skills the following year. Ongoing cumulative reviews as class warm-ups, centers that revisit skills from past lessons, and integrating review skills into our problem-solving tasks allow students to revisit skills throughout the school year to deepen their understanding, see connections between the skills they are learning, and have additional time, if needed, to master the skills.

Teaching Through Varied Instructional Formats

Whole-class instruction day after day cannot address our students' needs. We have long recognized that in the teaching of reading. We know we have students who read at lower levels and need more time and assistance to build their skills. We acknowledge that with different skill levels, they benefit from small-group instruction that can focus on their needs. We recognize that differentiated centers allow them to practice at a level that is right for them. But in math, many of us have clung to the whole-class approach. There are a multitude of reasons for varying instructional formats in our classrooms, including providing students with opportunities to explore concepts at different paces, experience lessons directed to their specific needs, and deepen their math thinking through collaboration with peers. Grouping formats might include:

- whole class
- teacher-led small groups
- collaborative groups/partners
- centers
- independent work.

The goal is to float in and out of these grouping formats as they best meet the needs of our students. On one day, students might work as a whole class as a skill is introduced, the next day there might be two activities going on simultaneously for varied ability levels within the classroom, and still another day some students may be working at centers while others are participating in teacher-led small groups. The varying formats allow us to select the one that best suits our needs at any point in time.

> *In the grade-level books, you will find a wealth of instructional ideas that can be used as whole-class or small-group lessons. Determine the grouping format that works best for your students.*

WHOLE-CLASS INSTRUCTION

Whole-class instruction has a place in the math classroom, but it is not the perfect instructional format we once believed. Whole-class instruction is definitely easier for teacher planning and allows us to introduce ideas to all students at the same time, but there are limitations to this often-used format. Some students in the class may not have the prior skills to fully grasp the concept being taught, making their participation unproductive and confusing. Others may already know the content, making them feel bored and disengaged. The large-group size limits teacher interaction, assessment options, and the effective use of some manipulatives. And students can be quietly disengaged from the learning when they are a part of a large group.

There are ways, however, to improve the effectiveness of whole-class instruction. Frequent turn-and-share opportunities throughout whole-class lessons keeps students engaged. Balancing a lesson with some whole-class portions and some small-group lessons provides students with short breaks, allowing for movement and a shift in focus.

TEACHER-LED SMALL GROUPS

Teacher-led small groups allow us to work with students who might be struggling with a particular topic or to extend a concept for students who are ready for a challenge. They allow us to more easily assess students as they talk and work and to provide opportunities for hands-on involvement when the materials or lesson would go more smoothly with fewer students. In small groups, students are able to have meaningful conversations with more active involvement. The ability to consistently talk about their thinking, combined with focusing questions and guidance from the teacher, allows students to analyze, interpret, and reflect on math ideas.

Small-group work might be a rotation in which all students have opportunities to meet with the teacher, but the content and delivery is modified to meet the needs of each group. So one group may be at a basic level, exploring the concept with hands-on materials, and another group is extending the concept to challenge the learners with a more advanced application of the skill. These small groups are not fixed. Students move in and out of the groups based on our formative assessment data because we recognize that a student who masters one skill quickly may need extra support with a different math skill.

Every group does not have to meet each day. Some teachers prefer rotations in which students are in small groups every other day, mixing in whole-class, partner, independent, and center options. And the time spent with each group does not have to be equal. Some groups may effectively accomplish the day's goals in 10–15 minutes, but others may require 20–25 minutes to adequately address the learning goal.

These groups are generally comprised of students with similar abilities, allowing the students to explore, discuss, and learn math at a level that is right for them. Because these groups are small, each session is filled with formative assessment. As we ask questions for students to answer, we are able to continue to probe for deeper answers and explanations. As we pose tasks for them to do, we are able to hear their partner talk or see their writing as they work right in front of us to complete the task. And because of the intimacy of the group, we are better able to determine when students might be ready to move to a different group.

Another type of teacher-led small group meets as the need arises during lessons. As teachers observe students working with partners, they may note that some students would benefit from additional guidance or may have misunderstandings that need to be clarified. Specific students might be invited to join a small group, or the teacher might invite any interested student to join. These are not preplanned groups, and the group often does the same task that other students in the class are doing, but rather than doing the task independently or with partners, the students engage in the task with teacher support. The teacher asks questions, shares models, offers suggestions, and provides specific feedback to advance their learning. The teacher gives these students the additional time and support they need.

A consideration when planning for group instruction is what the nonparticipating students are doing during small-group sessions. Meaningful math tasks, at varied ability levels, are critical for the success of small-group instruction. See Centers and Independent Work (page 165) for ideas on meaningful tasks.

Collaborative Groups/Partners

Collaborative teams provide students with the opportunity to work with their peers. Many students thrive on opportunities to share math ideas and work on math tasks with classmates. We have discussed the value of math talk (Chapter 4) and how it helps our students process their own ideas and gather new perspectives from listening to others.

Collaborative groups can be like-ability groups or mixed-ability groups, each having its benefits. Through mixed-ability groups, students have opportunities to pool their thinking. Students at lower levels are able to see and hear others' thinking, and research has supported the advantage for higher-level students as they are sometimes placed in roles of explaining and describing, helping them clarify their own understandings. But when students would benefit from addressing a skill at different levels of complexity, like-ability groups provide that opportunity. The teacher can simplify the task for one group and add complexity for another, giving each group a task that is at their instructional level (see Figure 5.10).

The success of these groups depends on students' understanding of the expectations for the task, as well as their abilities to effectively share their thinking. If one or two students seem to be doing all of the work, consider partner tasks instead of teams of 3–4 students. It is more difficult to disengage when only two students form a team.

For more on managing collaborative groups, see Chapter 4.

Figure 5.10 Team tasks are engaging and push students to take responsibility for their math discussions and investigations.

CENTERS AND INDEPENDENT WORK

Classroom centers offer another way to address students' varied needs. They provide engaging opportunities for students to explore math skills and concepts at different levels. Differentiated centers might provide practice for a previously taught skill, simply having different sets of cards to allow some to work with more complex data than others (see Figure 5.11). They might provide challenge tasks for students who have mastered a skill or concept, allowing them to explore the idea in greater depth. They might make use of concrete materials, visual models, or interactive technology (see Figure 5.12).

Center activities are provided throughout the grade-level books, including suggestions for modifying tasks.

Figure 5.11 While some students explore doubles facts at the center, others may be working on doubles plus 1 facts, allowing students to practice the skills that work for them.

Figure 5.12 Through the use of technology, this student is able to practice a skill at a level that makes sense for him.

Although independent tasks, particularly worksheets and workbook activities, have been overdone in math class, students do benefit from opportunities to do math on their own. Getting students involved in meaningful math tasks provides them with opportunities to process what they have learned, test their thinking, and apply their understanding. These tasks might be practice tasks but could also include tasks in which students illustrate key vocabulary, solve math problems, create math models, or write about their math thinking.

In most classrooms, the most frequent independent task centers around computational practice. Although students do need opportunities to practice their computational skills, the thoughtful selection of those computations determines whether the tasks are ultimately productive or not. When assigning this type of practice, there are some critical factors to consider:

- Quantity
    - Students benefit as much, or more, from shorter sets of thoughtfully chosen exercises.
    - Balance assignments by reducing the amount of computations, but adding a task that focuses on understanding (e.g., create a model, write a story problem for one of the computations, or explain the steps you used to solve it).
- Complexity level
    - Choose computations that match students' current needs and skills (neither beyond their level nor too far below it).
- Preparation for the task
    - Be sure that students know the skill well enough to perform it on their own before assigning it as an independent task. If it is a skill they were just introduced to, they may not be ready to do it alone.

Minimizing the quantity and selecting the correct level of computations may be simply a matter of having students circle specific item numbers on a worksheet page or cross off some items that appear on the page, or better yet, forgoing the worksheets altogether and simply posing a smaller quantity of computations. Focusing students' time and attention on the practice that works for them fosters engagement and builds motivation. No one wants to spend time doing tasks that feel like busy work.

And although practice tasks may be helpful, there are many other options for independent tasks. Consider having students gather data for an investigation (Chapter 1), revisit math vocabulary by completing word boxes or creating folded books (Chapter 4), draw models of math ideas (Chapter 3), solve or write story problems (Chapter 2), or write about their math experiences with explanations, justifications, or reflections (Chapter 4). Independent tasks should not be a vehicle to frustrate or turn off our students.

Modifying Math Tasks

Meaningful math tasks get students thinking about the math ideas they are exploring. For this to happen, it is vital that independent tasks are at an appropriate level. In reading, we use the terms *independent*, *frustrational*, and *instructional* to denote levels of reading material.

- *Independent level* is the level the student currently reads on. Students would not grow as readers if presented with only this level of material, because they are already able to read it.
- *Frustrational level* refers to material in which there are too many unknown words. Giving those materials to students frustrates them. They shut down because so much is unknown.
- *Instructional level* refers to materials with lots of known words, but enough that is unknown to present a doable challenge to students. These materials revisit what students know and introduce the unknown in quantities they can handle.

What are the implications for the math tasks we pose to our students?

A math textbook or workbook page may be at a frustrational level for some of our students, and an independent level for others. Our goal is to pose tasks that are at an instructional level, which means we are challenged to modify math tasks to make them appropriate for our students. Consider the following possibilities for modifying math tasks.

Tips for Modifying Math Tasks

Personalization

Many students turn off to math because the tasks feel like impersonal textbook exercises. It is amazing to see how students are captivated when their names appear in math problems or we substitute the generic restaurant name in the problem with a local restaurant or the sports team name with the local favorite. Students are drawn into the tasks when they are personalized, and when students are drawn into the task math learning happens.

Example: The students went to the fair . . .
Revision: Mrs. O'Connell's fourth graders went to the Benfield Fall Fair . . .

Readability

When faced with word problems, students' reading levels can interfere with their ability to do the math task. Although details motivate some students by making problems more interesting, they frustrate others who have limited reading abilities. Eliminating unnecessary words, or simply using a list format rather than a paragraph format, helps to simplify the text. Consider simplifying the reading level as in the following examples:

Example: Ellen packed 4 apples and 3 bananas for the picnic. How many pieces of fruit did she pack?
Revision:
   3 apples
   4 bananas
   How much fruit?

Example: Mrs. Bryant's class was studying health and fitness. Every student decided on a plan to get healthier. Danny decided to get more exercise. He rode his bike $2\frac{1}{4}$ miles each day for 9 days. How many miles did he ride?

Revision:

Danny rode his bike $2\frac{1}{4}$ miles each day for 9 days.
How many miles did he ride?

Length

For students who are anxious about or lack confidence with math tasks, one look at the quantity of items on a page can cause them to shut down. Try the following to motivate them to tackle the task without being turned off by the length of it.

- Scale It Down—Reduce the number of computations or problems that students must complete depending on their skills and abilities. You might circle the computations on a worksheet that students should complete or cross off any that are not necessary for them to complete.
- Cut It Out—Consider cutting assignment sheets in half and giving the first part to all students. As students finish the first half, individually provide them with part two of the task. This allows you to quickly scan their work and step in to support them if they are off track, before they proceed to the second part of the task.

Complexity of Data

A simple way to modify math tasks is by adjusting the data. Fewer pieces of data, or friendlier numbers, simplify tasks. Additional pieces of data, or less-friendly numbers, add complexity. See the following examples:

Example: At the zoo, Ellen saw 5 zebras, 4 hippos, and 2 elephants. How many animals did she see? (Addition includes three addends.)

Revision with simpler data: At the zoo, Ellen saw 5 zebras and 4 hippos. How many animals did she see? (Three addends become two addends.)

Revision with more complex data: At the zoo, Ellen saw 5 zebras, 7 hippos, and 10 elephants. How many animals did she see? (One of the three single-digit addends is replaced with a 10.)

Example: Central School has 552 students. Hilltop School has 376 students. How many more students go to Central School? (Task requires subtraction with regrouping in two places.)

Revision with simpler data: Central School has 559 students. Hilltop School has 376 students. How many more students go to Central School? (Task requires subtraction with regrouping in one place.)

Revision with more complex data: Central School has 1,103 students. Hilltop School has 876 students. How many more students go to Central School? (Task requires subtraction with regrouping in two places with larger numbers, including subtraction across a 0.)

Additional Steps

Inserting additional steps and challenging students with missing data are simple ways to extend math tasks. Consider the following:

Example: Kim baked 3 dozen cookies for the party. Kim's friends ate $\frac{3}{4}$ of them. How many cookies were left?

continues

Revision: Kim baked 3 dozen cookies for the party. Kim's friends ate $\frac{3}{4}$ of them and then Kim's little brother ate 2 more. How many cookies were left? (The additional data make this a two-step problem.)

Alternate revision: Kim baked 3 dozen cookies for the party. Kim's friends ate $\frac{3}{4}$ of them and then Kim's little brother ate $\frac{1}{3}$ of what was left. How many cookies were left? (The additional step in this version requires another fraction computation.)

Example: Find the area of a rectangle that is 8 cm wide and 16 cm long.

Revision: Find the area of a rectangle. Its width is 8 cm and its length is double its width. (The missing data about the length make it a two-step task.)

Modifying Support

One way to modify math tasks is by adjusting the actual task, but another option is to adjust the type and amount of support given to students. This support might be adjustments of time or output methods, personal support by the teacher or a classmate, or support in the form of tools that allow them to more effectively perform the math task. Consider the following possibilities:

- Time—For students who work at a slower pace, consider increasing the time given to complete an assignment. For quick finishers, consider adding a second tier to an activity to extend the concept.
- Checkpoints—Consider increasing the amount of assistance given to a student through personal checkpoints to review the student's work (e.g., the student brings the first three completed computations to the teacher to check before moving on to others).
- Peer Support—Assign a peer buddy to answer questions as needed during the task.
- Tools—Allow the student to use tools as needed (e.g., manipulatives, hundred charts, multiplication tables, or calculators).
- Output—Modify how the student shows understanding (i.e., instead of requiring the student to answer a problem in writing, allow the student to respond verbally, or allow the student to list items rather than write complete paragraphs). You might increase the size of the work space for some students who write large or tend to use lots of models to show their work.

The Value of Choice

The ability to choose a math task is appealing to many students. Although all task options should relate to key skills and concepts so that students delve into similar content, varied tasks allow students to explore ideas and show their understanding in ways that match their strengths, interests, needs, and learning styles. Consider the following examples:

TOPIC: CHARACTERISTICS OF QUADRILATERALS

Possible math tasks:

- Use toothpicks, pipe cleaners, or Wikki Stix® to create models of quadrilaterals. Label each one with its name and characteristics. (for hands-on learners)
- Create a book about quadrilaterals. Use words, pictures, and examples to show what you know about each quadrilateral. (for visual learners who like to create books and illustrate their ideas)
- Work with a team to demonstrate quadrilaterals. Explain each one, and its characteristics, to the class as you create the shape. (for kinesthetic learners who like to move as they learn)
- Work with a partner to create a quadrilateral poster. Find pictures in the newspaper or magazine that show various quadrilaterals and cut, paste, and label each one to create the poster. Label each with the characteristics of the quadrilateral. Share the poster with the class. (for visual learners and those who like to explore applications of a skill)
- Write some true-or-false statements about the characteristics of quadrilaterals. Create an answer key to explain whether each statement is true or false and why. (for linguistic learners, those who like to work independently, and those who enjoy creating puzzles and games)
- Compare and contrast the characteristics of three different quadrilaterals. Tell how they are alike and different. (for analytical thinkers)

TOPIC: ADDITION OF FRACTIONS WITH UNLIKE DENOMINATORS

Possible math tasks:

- Create a sequence chain to show the steps for adding fractions with unlike denominators. (for the step-by-step procedural student)
- With a partner, write a list of important tips for adding fractions with unlike denominators. (for the student who enjoys writing about their ideas)
- Compare adding fractions with like denominators to adding fractions with unlike denominators. How are the processes alike? How are the processes different? (for the analytical student)
- Write a letter convincing someone that adding fractions with unlike denominators is an important skill to know. Tell what you must know to be able to add these fractions. Give an example of when you might need to do it. (for the student who likes to work independently)
- Make up some true-or-false statements about adding fractions with unlike denominators. Create an answer key to explain whether each statement is true or false and why. (for the student who likes creating puzzles or games)

Many teachers create choice boards to display the possible projects (e.g., a variety of tasks recorded on index cards and displayed in hanging pockets). Students select a task card that suits their style and interest and then work on the task during center or independent work time. The ability to select a task, even if only given two or three choices, is a strong motivator and a great way to adapt tasks to various students' styles and interests.

Tips for Supporting All Learners

Supporting Learners Through Visual Experiences

- Use pictures, charts, maps, and graphs whenever possible.
- Demonstrate procedures and illustrate concepts using visual tools like interactive whiteboards or document cameras.
- When posting vocabulary words, include diagrams whenever possible.
- Encourage students to draw pictures/diagrams as they record their ideas.
- Have students highlight or underline key ideas.
- Place worksheets in page protectors and allow students to write on the plastic cover with dry erase markers.
- Have students create models for word problems.
- Use a variety of media (computers, video) in lessons.
- Share illustrated books that support math concepts.
- Emphasize illustrations and diagrams in the math text.
- Encourage students to use pictures, diagrams, examples, and/or representations to show what they know.

Supporting Learners Through Auditory Experiences

- Provide lots of class discussions and group work to discuss math ideas.
- Use a think-aloud technique to talk through solving problems or doing procedures.
- Allow students to show their understanding through presentations.
- Allow students to read text, problems, procedures, or solutions aloud.
- Allow some students to verbalize responses rather than writing them.
- Pair students to read and work on problems together or to periodically discuss their progress with their partner.
- Have students create songs, poems, or mnemonics to aid memorization.
- Assign peer buddies or cross-grade-level tutors to provide some extra support or consider training "home partners" (parents or other relatives) to provide additional support at home.

Supporting Learners Through Kinesthetic Experiences

- Include movement whenever possible (e.g., lineups to sequence numbers, group formations to show geometric shapes).
- Allow students to work in a standing position.
- Frequently use manipulatives to allow students to visualize concepts (e.g., geoboards to show geometric shapes, base-ten blocks to show place value, pattern blocks to explore fractions).
- Have students create interactive study guides by folding paper into sections and recording ideas in each section.
- Help students line up numbers for computations by turning loose-leaf paper on its side so the lines form columns or by using graph paper.
- Allow students to move to centers to work on hands-on activities.
- Act out story problems.
- Create physical graphs with students standing in for the data.
- Provide interactive games using dice, spinners, cards, and so on to illustrate and practice math skills.

- Have toolboxes of materials (e.g., colored chips, cubes, calculators, paper and pencil) available in the classroom to allow students to access materials that might assist them in completing the task.
- Encourage every-pupil-response techniques by using pinch cards or individual dry erase boards.
- Create review puzzles by cutting questions and answers apart and having students match the correct answer to each question.

Modifying Instruction for English Language Learners

Many of the ideas we have already discussed can also support English language learners in the math classroom. Consider the advantages for these students when manipulatives, visuals, discussions, and vocabulary activities are a regular part of our math teaching.

Engaging students in math talk is critical. We learn a language by speaking it and listening to it being spoken. Engage English language learners in partner and small-group activities and provide multiple opportunities for them to talk about math. Allow them to work with partners during math tasks to ask questions or clarify directions. And whenever possible, allow students to express their ideas in their home language.

In Chapter 4, we discussed the importance of developing the language of math. Although this is important for all students, it is particularly important for English language learners. The vocabulary tasks highlighted in Chapter 4, including the use of Math Talk charts to highlight key vocabulary, should be an ongoing part of our math instruction. Using sorting and categorizing activities, such as sort and label and word web, are particularly helpful as they focus students on the similarities and differences between certain math words and concepts. And a focus on vocabulary should extend beyond content vocabulary to include academic words like the following: *describe, justify, persuade, analyze, prove, simplify, retell, compare/contrast, order, identify, justify, define, solve, sort*, and *model*. These words describe the actions of mathematicians and allow students to successfully interpret and complete math tasks.

The use of models in math class (Chapter 3) provides opportunities for students to talk about and explore math concepts through manipulative experiences and visual representations. Encouraging students to create visuals to go along with concepts helps them process the language along with the math ideas. And as we use visual images to support our verbal explanations, students are better able to access the ideas we are teaching.

Students who are just beginning to develop an understanding of the English language can experience a great deal of anxiety related to the reading of math problems and tasks. Encouraging collaborative reading, reading problems or directions with a partner, relieves student anxiety and allows them to figure out what the problem or task is asking of them. And creating models to visualize and comprehend problems takes the emphasis away from the words and on to the models and problem data.

Assessing students' understanding is paramount for our English learners, yet they may have difficulty with paper-and-pencil tasks, not truly showing what they know. Allowing them to tell or demonstrate their understanding through interviews can give us more accurate assessment information, so we are able to tailor our instruction to meet their needs.

Students come to us with different knowledge and skills, move at different paces, and learn in different ways. We are constantly challenged to figure out what they know about a particular math topic and then are further challenged to find ways to extend that understanding through the lessons we design and the teaching practices we employ. Through our formative assessment options and our varied teaching practices, formats, and tasks, we let our students guide our teaching.

 Scan this QR code or visit http://hein.pub/MathinPractice to see videos related to assessment and differentiation and to access additional online resources (use keycode MIPGT).

Study Group Questions

1. What is the goal of formative assessment?
2. What does formative assessment look like in K–5 classrooms?
3. How can you be sure your formative assessments provide you with enough depth to determine next steps?
4. What are the advantages and disadvantages of different formative assessment options?
5. What does feedback look like in your math classroom?
6. How do you decide whether to give feedback to individuals, to a small group, or to the whole class?
7. In what ways can we modify instruction to make it accessible for different types and levels of learners?
8. What are the advantages and disadvantages of different grouping formats? How do we decide which one to use?
9. Why modify math tasks? In what ways can we modify them?

Conclusion

Our students' experiences in K–5 classrooms build the foundation for their success in mathematics at the middle grades and beyond. Although our students are introduced to foundational skills and concepts during the elementary years, K–5 math is so much more than an accumulation of skills. During the K–5 years, our students learn to investigate, observe, conjecture, reconsider, and generalize about math ideas. They learn how math works; develop an understanding of number concepts; learn to examine, explore, and solve problems; acquire methods for communicating their understanding; and improve their mathematical reasoning. And during these years, if our students gain confidence in their math abilities and develop a positive disposition about mathematics, they have the foundation to move forward in their study of mathematics.

As teachers, we have seen a change in the definition of mathematical proficiency to reach far beyond computational skills. We have witnessed new standards that focus on understanding and application. And we acknowledge that past teaching practices are not well matched to these new expectations for our students. It is time to readjust our teaching practices to better suit these new expectations.

Although standards, curricula, and lesson plans can guide change, the real change, the change that matters most to our students, begins with us. We are the teachers of mathematics, the ones that transform words on a page into real lessons. We are the ones who listen to students and adapt and modify tasks to meet their needs. We are the ones who must decide on the spot how to reframe concepts, readjust lessons, or revisit skills. We are the ones who must find ways to continue to assess and adjust our teaching as we monitor and advance students' skills.

The expectations for our students have changed, and so our teaching practices must change along with them. We must craft a new image of what a teacher of elementary math looks like and sounds like.

- **Teachers of K–5 mathematics know math content**—not just rules and math facts, but a deep understanding of the concepts being taught. They understand the connections between math ideas and understand why rules work.
- **Teachers of K–5 mathematics know that math is active.** They know the importance of students discovering their own insights and so find ways to guide their students toward discovering critical math ideas. Rather than telling their students rules, or having them complete endless worksheets, they make sure their students are actively involved in doing math and are engaged in making sense of math ideas.
- **Teachers of K–5 mathematics recognize that students learn in different ways** and are able to illustrate and explain math ideas in a variety of ways. They ask thoughtful questions, help students make connections between ideas, support math talk, and select appropriate learning tools.
- **Teachers of K–5 mathematics recognize that identifying what their students know is foundational to making informed decisions about their instruction.** They recognize that

they may need to provide additional time and support for some and extensions for others (and that the same student may be in both categories depending on the math topic).

- **Teachers of K–5 mathematics know the importance of developing a positive disposition.** They inspire confidence and make their students feel capable in math. They celebrate discoveries and successes. They know that if their students believe they can learn, they will learn.

We have shifted our focus from teacher-directed to student-directed classrooms. We have begun to listen to our students and consider their knowledge, skills, and learning styles to offer the best teaching possible. We have begun to think of mathematics as something to be experienced rather than something to be memorized.

In the Introduction, we identified three steps to consider as we transition our teaching practices to meet the expectations for today's elementary students.

1. Update our beliefs about math. Have we accepted that as math expectations for our students change, our teaching practices must change along with them?
2. Rediscover math content. Have we acknowledged that we were not taught to understand math skills and concepts and may need to revisit those skills and concepts to teach our students to understand them?
3. Modify our instruction to match our new beliefs and content understandings. Have we identified ways we can modify our teaching to help our students meet their goals?

As you reflect on your math teaching, consider shifts, whether large or small, that enrich your approach to teaching mathematics. How will your students look back on their experiences in your math classroom? Will they remember a teacher who helped them discover math insights, make sense of math ideas, and develop a love of math?

Questions and Answers

Is Math in Practice a curriculum?

No. This series is meant to fit with any curriculum and to allow you to access strategies and activities based on whatever standards you are teaching. Although Math in Practice does provide a wealth of activities for teaching math, it is intended to be much more than a collection of teaching ideas. It is designed to help you gain greater insight into the math you are teaching and discover more ways to teach it. It is filled with important tips and strategies for helping students better understand critical math skills and concepts.

How are the grade-level books connected to the Guide for Teachers?

Math in Practice: A Guide for Teachers explores teaching strategies that enhance students' understanding of mathematics. The grade-level books illustrate those teaching strategies with specific activities that focus on grade-level math standards. In many places throughout the grade-level books, you will notice notes that refer you back to the *Guide for Teachers* for more information on the instructional strategy.

Are the modules in the grade-level books meant to be teaching units?

No. The modules are organized to allow teachers to easily access information about a math topic. They are not intended to be teaching units for students. In fact, students will retain information better if they revisit it throughout the year (e.g., you might explore fractions early in the year, then revisit the topic later in the year to extend the ideas). Revisiting modules throughout the year allows you to address the same math topic at different levels.

Are the modules in the grade-level books meant to be done in order?

No. Your district will likely have a pacing guide for you to follow. You can jump in and out of modules as needed but will want to consider the prior skills your students will need as they explore a particular math topic.

There are two activity sections in each module. What is the difference between them?

In each module you will find two sections: Ideas for Instruction and Assessment and Additional Ideas for Support and Practice.

The Ideas for Instruction and Assessment section contains ideas that can be easily developed into lessons. This section contains major teaching points and explores a variety of ways to help students understand a skill or concept. Most of the activities also have assessment components as you observe your students, listen to their explanations, and review their work. In addition, specific formative assessment tasks are highlighted in this section.

The Additional Ideas for Support and Practice section contains suggestions for students who may need additional exposure to the skill, as well as a variety of practice tasks and challenge tasks, including center activities that provide meaningful practice.

A few modules in grades 1–3 that focus on basic math facts, have a different structure. These modules include Ideas for Instruction and Assessment as in the other modules, but instead of the Additional Ideas for Support and Practice section, these modules contain a variety of activities intended to build students' fluency with the basic facts.

How can I get insight into the critical math ideas in each module?

At the start of each module is a section called About the Math in which the key math ideas are discussed, including situating the math in a learning progression (what students should have learned the previous year and what they will be learning the following year). This can help you identify skills your students may need additional practice with; you can refer to previous grade-level books for ideas to help you build those prerequisite skills and understandings.

What kinds of teaching supports are found in the lesson ideas?

One of the most significant components of math teaching is the questions we ask our students. Our questions have the power to advance their thinking; students' answers provide us with critical assessment information. To get you thinking about the types of questions you might ask related to a specific math skill, we have generated questions for you to consider. Asking pairs to discuss the questions, then having students share their thinking with the class, ensures that all students are thinking about the key ideas of the lesson.

You will also find notes that address typical errors and misconceptions. Recognizing those typical errors allows us to design our teaching to address them and to be vigilant as we listen and watch our students at work.

You'll also see general teaching notes that highlight opportunities for differentiation, specific examples of the pedagogical strategies from the *Guide for Teachers*, and other hints and suggestions from teachers who have used these activities.

I noticed some lessons labeled Thinking Through a Lesson. What is different about these lessons?

Thinking Through a Lesson sections contain reflective lessons that allow you to hear the thinking of the teacher who designed the activity. In each module, you will find one of these lessons that contains multiple teacher notes to explain the teaching choices, talk about possible misconceptions, or share tips for supporting learners. In these lessons, anticipated student responses are included to give you an idea of the type of math talk that is likely to occur during the lessons. In addition, the pertinent Standards for Mathematical Practice are indicated to allow you to reflect on how these critical standards are integrated into the lesson.

What is available in the online resources?

There are a wealth of online resources available including recording sheets, center activity templates, spinners and other tools, and additional problem-solving tasks related to each module. Throughout the grade-level books, you will notice small images indicating some of these resources; however, take the time to explore the online resources because there is more there than can be shown in the grade-level books.

How can I modify the online activities?

Many of the online resources are in Microsoft Word format, so they can be used with interactive whiteboards and are easily customized to meet your students' needs. You might decide to personalize the tasks with your students' names, modify the data to make the problem simpler or more complex, or delete sections to shorten the task. The resources are templates that can be used as is or modified in any way that works for your students.

References

Black, Paul, and Dylan Wiliam. 1998. "Inside the Black Box: Raising Standards through Classroom Assessment." *Phi Delta Kappan* (October): 139–48.

Bransford, John D., Ann L. Brown, and Rodney R. Cocking (Eds.). 1999. *How People Learn: Brain, Mind, Experience, and School.* Washington, DC: National Academy Press.

Brown, Margaret Wise. 1999. *The Important Book.* New York: HarperCollins.

Carpenter, Thomas, Megan Loef Franke, and Linda Levi. 2003. *Thinking Mathematically: Integrating Arithmetic and Algebra in Elementary School.* Portsmouth, NH: Heinemann.

Chapin, Suzanne H., Catherine O'Connor, and Nancy Canavan Anderson. 2009. *Classroom Discussions: Using Math Talk to Help Students Learn.* Sausalito, CA: Math Solutions.

Crespo, Sandra. 2000. "Seeing More Than Right and Wrong Answers: Prospective Teachers' Interpretations of Students' Mathematical Work." *Journal of Mathematics Teacher Education* 3 (2): 155–81.

Fennema, Elizabeth, and Thomas A. Romberg. 1999. *Mathematics Classrooms That Promote Understanding.* Mahwah, NJ: Erlbaum.

Fosnot, Catherine Twomey, and William Jacob. 2010. *Young Mathematicians at Work: Constructing Algebra.* Portsmouth, NH: Heinemann.

Fuson, Karen C., Mindy Kalchman, and John D. Bransford. 2005. "Mathematical Understanding: An Introduction." In *How Students Learn: History, Mathematics, and Science in the Classroom*, edited by Suzanne Donovan and John D. Bransford, Committee on How People Learn: A Targeted Report for Teachers, National Research Council, 217–56. Washington, DC: National Academies Press.

Goldin, Gerald. 2003. "Representation in School Mathematics: A Unifying Research Perspective." In *A Research Companion to Principles and Standards for School Mathematics*, edited by Jeremy Kilpatrick, W. Gary Martin, and Deborah Schifter, 275–85. Reston, VA: NCTM.

Greeno, James G., and Rogers P. Hall. 1997. "Practicing Representation: Learning With and About Representational Forms." *Phi Delta Kappan* 78 (5): 361–67.

Guinness World Records. 2015. *Guinness World Records 2016.* New York: Guinness World Records.

Hattie, John. 2008. *Visible Learning: A Synthesis of Over 800 Meta-Analyses Relating to Achievement.* New York: Routledge.

Hiebert, James. 2003. "What Research Says About the NCTM Standards." In *A Research Companion to Principles and Standards for School Mathematics*, edited by Jeremy Kilpatrick, W. Gary Martin, and Deborah Schifter, 5–23. Reston, VA: NCTM.

Leinwand, Steven. 2012. *Sensible Mathematics, 2d ed.: A Guide for School Leaders in the Era of Common Core State Standards.* Portsmouth, NH: Heinemann.

Marzano, Robert J., Debra J. Pickering, and Jane E. Pollock. 2001. *Classroom Instruction That Works: Research-Based Strategies for Increasing Student Achievement.* Alexandria, VA: Association for Supervision and Curriculum Development.

Monk, Stephen, and TERC. 2003. "Representation in School Mathematics: Learning to Graph and Graphing to Learn." In *A Research Companion to Principles and Standards for School Mathematics*, edited by Jeremy Kilpatrick, W. Gary Martin, and Deborah Schifter, 250–62. Reston, VA: NCTM.

National Geographic Kids. 2012. *5000 Awesome Facts (About Everything)!* Washington, DC: National Geographic Children's Books.

———. 2014. *The National Geographic Kids Almanac 2015.* Washington, DC: National Geographic Children's Books.

National Council of Teachers of Mathematics. 1995. *Assessment Standards for School Mathematics.* Reston, VA: NCTM.

———. 2000. *Principles and Standards for School Mathematics.* Reston, VA: NCTM.

———. 2014. *Principles to Actions: Ensuring Mathematical Success for All.* Reston, VA: NCTM.

National Council of Supervisors of Mathematics. 2014. *It's Time: Themes and Imperatives for Mathematics Education.* Bloomington, IN: Solution Tree Press.

National Governors Association Center for Best Practices and Council of Chief State School Officers. 2010. *Common Core State Standards for Mathematics.* Accessed on December 9, 2015. www.corestandards.org/assets/CCSSI_Math%20Standards.pdf.

National Research Council. 2009. *Mathematics Learning in Early Childhood: Paths Toward Excellence and Equity*, edited by Christopher T. Cross, Taneisha A. Woods, and Heidi Schweingruber, Committee on Early Childhood Mathematics, Center for Education, Division of Behavioral and Social Sciences and Education. Washington, DC: National Academies Press.

O'Connell, Susan R. 2005. *Now I Get It: Strategies for Building Confident and Competent Mathematicians, K–6.* Heinemann: Portsmouth, NH.

Polya, George. 2004. *How to Solve It: A New Aspect of Mathematical Method.* Princeton, NJ: Princeton University Press.

Smith, Stephen. 2003. "Representation in School Mathematics: Children's Representations of Problems." In *A Research Companion to Principles and Standards for School Mathematics*, edited by Jeremy Kilpatrick, W. Gary Martin, and Deborah Schifter, 263–74. Reston, VA: NCTM.

Spangler, Denise A., JiSun Kim, Dionne Cross, Hulya Kilic, F. Asli Iscimen, and Diana Swanagan. 2014. "Using Rich Tasks to Promote Discourse." In *Using Research to Improve Instruction 2014*, edited by Karen Karp and Amy Roth McDuffie. Reston, VA: NCTM.

Stein, Mary Kay, and Margaret S. Smith. 2011. *5 Practices for Orchestrating Productive Mathematics Discussions*. Reston, VA and Thousand Oaks, CA: NCTM and Corwin Press.

Strong, Richard, Ed Thomas, Matthew Perini, and Harvey Silver. 2004. "Creating a Differentiated Mathematics Classroom." *Educational Leadership* (February): 73–78.

Time for Kids. 2014. *Time for Kids Almanac 2015*. New York: Time for Kids.

Tomlinson, Carol Ann. 2014. *The Differentiated Classroom: Responding to the Needs of All Learners, 2d ed.* Alexandria, VA: Association for Supervision and Curriculum Development.

Van de Walle, John A., and LouAnn Lovin. 2006. *Teaching Student-Centered Mathematics Grades 3–5*. New York: Pearson.

Wiliam, Dylan. 2007. "Keeping Learning on Track: Classroom Assessment and the Regulation of Learning." In *Second Handbook of Mathematics Teaching and Learning*, edited by Frank K. Lester, Jr., 1053–98. Charlotte, NC: Information Age; Reston, VA: National Council of Teachers of Mathematics.